MANICHAEISM

and Satanic Child Abuse

JULEON SCHINS

Manichaeism and Satanic Child Abuse

© 2019 by Juleon Schins. All rights reserved.

No part of this publication may be reproduced, stored in a retrieval system or transmitted in any way by any means, electronic, mechanical, photocopy, recording or otherwise without the prior permission of the author except as provided by US copyright law.

ISBN 978-1-64550-163-3 (Paperback)

CONTENTS

Introduction: Satanic Child Abuse   i

Chapter 1   History   1
Chapter 2   Statistics   43
Chapter 3   Survivors   57

Appendices   Contents A1 ad A2   75
Epilogue   Original Sin   77

Commedia: Inferno

di Dante Alighieri[1]
Canto XVII, 10-15, 25-27

La faccia sua era faccia d'uom giusto,
tanto benigna avea di fuor la pelle,
e d'un serpente tutto l'altro fusto

due branche avea pilose insin l'ascelle;
lo dosso e 'l petto e ambedue le coste
dipinti avea di nodi e di rotelle.

Nel vano tutta sua coda guizzava,
torcendo in sù la venenosa forca
ch'a guisa di scorpion la punta armava.

---

[1] 1285-1321

Comedy: Hell

by Dante Alighieri
Chant XVII, 10-15, 25-27

His face was the face of a saintly person,
so placid was the surface of the skin,
but his whole trunk was the shape of a snake

he had two paws, with hair up to his armpits;
his back and breasts and both of his flanks
were painted gaudily with knots and loops.

Out in the void all his tail stretched quivering,
twisting in the air its poisonous fork
which had a tip armed like a scorpion's.

This book is part of a 2019 decalogue consisting of

- Sign of Times: Music Anthology and Lyric Analysis
- Hollywood Misogyny
- Beginners' Guide to the FED: Why it is Unique on our Planet
- The Kennedy Kurse: Four Obvious Konnektions
- Manichaeism and Satanic Child Abuse
- Progressive Intolerance: Last Stop Before Hitler
- Patriotic Ingenuousness
- Deism versus Theism: 2-7 in the Scientific Arena of the 20th Century
- Feminine Feminist: A Missing Link Eluding Discovery
- The Snake: Three Millennia of Anti-Semitism

Dedicated to Pope Francis
with Filial Affection

INTRODUCTION
Satanic Child Abuse

Not all religions are the same, even though most non-believers think of them like that. These non-believers often tell you, without even blinking, that all wars are fundamentally due to religious issues. One concludes that, according to the latter kings of logic, all wars are due to people fighting over the supremacy of a single religion! In the remainder of this book I assume that the reader has won such state of profound ignorance, or brainwashing, as you wish to call it. This book is written for people who understand that wars are *always directly* about power, and indirectly about means to get there: money, rare material resources, technology, military innovation, and, if required, supremacy of religions. That is to say, stirring up different religious groups one against the other is *never, nor has ever been, a cause of war*, but always a mere means in the hands of warlords to win their war.

After the earliest, eastern, Christian Councils, most eastern Christians had embraced Manichaeism for merely political reasons. Their emperor obviously could not suffer that his people looked to the west for religious matters, in very much the same way as Anglican, Lutheran, and Calvinist leaders would not suffer from their people looking south for religious matters.

Manichaeism slowly penetrated all of eastern Christianity. A famous follower went by the name of Augustine (354-430) of Hippo Regius, an "Algerian" city (Annaba) that was devastated shortly after his death by the Vandals. They apparently had a problem with Christianity. It was but one phase in the violent disappearance of Christianity in Northern Africa: exactly the same kind of phenomenon we presently witness in the Middle East. Then it was the Vandals, today it is the Israeli's.

Because Augustine suspected a lack of consistency in Manichaeism, he never made it beyond the lowest follower degree, that of *auditor*. His decision to definitively quit Manichaeism fell after having dined with the highest authority of Manichaeism, who was quite impressed by Augustine's oratory and sophistic skills. On his turn, Augustine revered the personality and teaching of a Christian Bishop, Aurelius Ambrose (Saint Ambrose) of Milan, made Bishop by mere popular acclamation in 374.[2] The seed had been thrown, and within a decade

---

[2] This is quite unique in the Catholic Church, which used to be a champion of rigor in its procedures. For more recent applications, read about Bergoglio's systematic blundering in China, e.g., by former Bishop Yen of Singapore.

Augustine converted to Christianity. Besides being orator by profession, Augustine was a gifted theologian – and not a sophistic one at that. The eastern ("Orthodox") Church rejected his most controversial doctrine, to wit, that the Holy Ghost proceeds from *both* Father and Son (*filioque* in the official western creed), as said above, mostly for political reasons. Disputed teachings in Rome include his development of original sin, his doctrine of grace, and that of predestination. Present-day Catholicism accepts most of his theology, though with some circumstance-modifications on his exact phrasing concerning grace, free will, and predestination, all regarded as an overreaction to Pelagianism.[3]

As a convert from Manichaeism and a gifted orator, Augustine was one of the few in the history of Christianity, able to explain the main difference between Christianity and Manichaeism to a large, non-specialized public. Even though the explanation was quite academic, the practical consequences were huge. Manichaeism also overreacted to Augustine: first it regarded carnal sin as unforgivable, and later it turned into a cult of sexual debauchery.

Unique among all other extant religions, Christianity considered satan as a mere *creature of God*,[4] while all

---

[3] Pelagius taught that human free will had the power to access supernatural virtues without divine grace. To hold such an opinion today, is identical to not being Catholic.

[4] According to the "Catechism of the Catholic Church", as of to

other religions thought of good and evil as two balanced principles, in permanent fight against one another. For Christianity, *evil was merely an expression of "theological emptiness or absence"; specifically, lack of love*. God being Infinitely Perfect Love and Free Will, *all evil must be due to a free created being's not being able to choose for freely loving God.*[5] *Evil is a mere inability to grasp a treasure*. Obviously, the actions of a free creature are positive and actual. That is consequence of satan's free will, which God respects as all other created free decisions. However, for a creature the deepest inner motivation to want to perform an evil act, is a mere absence of free will to grasp the good. It is certainly not an overabundance of free will to grasp evil. The latter view

---

    date many Catholic theologians hold that satan was God's first creature, the creature that resembled God as much as possible, without incurring into inconsistency. The "Catechism of the Catholic Church", is unique among all religions, as it does not only state some central pillars of belief, but it explains the creed in its tiniest details. This is conspicuously not the case for the other two monotheistic religions: Judaism and Islam, nor for all Churches split off the Catholic branch.

5 Excuse my duplication: to "choose" or to "will" imply, by definition, the concept of such a high degree of liberty, or freedom, that the chooser is the only source of the chosen act. That is to say, the free being is a mini-god with creative power, though only concerning its own will. For example, a prisoner is philosophically as free as any non-prisoner. Circumstances determine whether a free being is actually able "to realize" her choice, or better said, to see her choice realized.

may hold as many religions as one pleases, though not for Catholicism, as the latter is self-declaredly self-consistent.

This Catholic teaching might be *understandably consistent*, though it must necessarily be limited in its degree *of penetrability or inclusiveness*. That is to say: on one hand, it should be impossible to argue the contradiction between any two elements of unfaultable Catholic doctrine, while on the other, it should be impossible to comprehend the consistency of that very doctrine as a whole. This age-old Catholic view is nothing but a theological predecessor of the 20th century number-theoretical discovery by Einstein's Austrian friend Kurt Gödel.[6] The same holds for Angels, too: they cannot argue any internal contradiction, and at the time, are unable to oversee the consistency of all truth. God is perfectly rational but *infinitely incomprehensible*, and nothing prevents His creation to carry signs of its Creator. Either God is infinitely superior to his creatures, and therefore not fully comprehensible to them, or He is not, thus being nothing more than an intelligent angel. Hence, *Catholic doctrine is the only consistent way to conceive God with his attributes of Infinite Love, Justice, Mercy, Free Will, Intelligence, Self-Consistency, and Impenetrability.*[7]

---

6 See my book "Deism versus Theism" for more detailed information about Kurt Gödel's startling discovery.
7 Atheists have but one axiom: there is no such thing as an incomprehensible being. Too bad, this is a negative axiom,

Somewhat less kindly formulated, all other religious systems, which claim the same attributes for their god, do so inconsistently.

Although the dictionary has "Satan" with an initial capital, for being a person's name, in this book I prefer to use "satan", for the mere purpose of denying him any kind of appreciation: I would rather write "little cozy satan" than use an appreciative title. After all, he is but a barking dog chained to a post. Only those people get bitten who venture closer than they should, with the length of the dog's line clearly visible to everybody.[8]

By way of summary, the answer to the question "how can there be evil in God's created world, assuming that God is Infinitely Loving, Just, Merciful, Free, Intelligent, Self-Consistent, and Impenetrable", is that God respects the free decisions of all his creatures, including the "social effects" that evil among higher creatures might have on lower ones. Since humans are infinitely inferior to the satan, their free will is so, as well.[9] In Catholic terms, "free will" is a creature's ability to create one's choice for or against God out of nothing. In contrast to the Calvinistic

---

    which by consistency implies that there cannot exist a natural argument of reasonability.
8   The length of the line is made known to oneself by one's own conscience.
9   Who doubts about the existence of human freedom (whether in prison or outside) is encouraged to throw this book into the garbage can now

teaching of predestination, God does not produce a "free choice" for any of his free creatures.[10] His being the creator of free choice, he obviously (by necessity of self-consistency) knows on forehand what a creature is going to do, though without being the author of a creature's free act. Thinking otherwise, for example, that God's foreknowledge is somehow understandably comparable to human foreknowledge (as in Calvin's double predestination), is inconsistent.

Due to their enormous strength of free will, all angels (including cozy satan) are able to manifest their eternally valid choice – for or against God – in a unique act on their own timeline.[11] On the other hand, humans need a spatio-temporal lifetime to reach a definitive choice.

Catholic Tradition believes that satan "fell" into his abysm when confronted with God's wish to create the Virgin Mary. He was a kind of primordial sexist but asexual macho, as he could not grasp how a human being

---

[10] Animals are not included. God loves them, however, and no doubt they will be in Heaven, too, but not for their own sake (as animals do not understand anything at all), though for the sake of human happiness.

[11] The Angelic timeline has nothing whatsoever in common with Einstein's relativity: Angels are self-consistent, yet incomprehensible to humans. For the sake of consistency, the degree of angelic incomprehensibility is infinitely lower than God's, yet still infinitely higher than that of humans (which is already incomprehensible to humans). No problem here, Angels do not fully understand their essence, either.

(and a female one at that)[12] could be elevated in dignity above all Angels, to the point of becoming their only Queen. This was, quite understandably, a heavy blow for the most beautiful of creatures.[13] Whence satan refused God's offer, and created his own cozy place, better known by the name of hell. According the Catholic creed, *hell is not a four-dimensional "Einsteinian space-time", but a mere fixation of one's will never to see God*. God respects this will, and allows devils to fight one another, while torturing humans up to a maximum point determined by God's mercy. A careful reader might ask who the hell has the power to torture satan, as he is untouchable in hell. Well, certainly not God Himself, as He is only able to do good. The satan is indeed untouchable in hell, even if all fallen angels would conspire to attack him.

Yet his pain is the worst of all. It is simply the consequence of his choice never to see God. As all creatures cannot be created (by mere consistency) for anything but seeing and loving God in seeing Him, the satan suffers God's absence the most of all creatures. That is because of his supreme beauty, intelligence, and will strength: the satan necessarily conceives the inability to

---

12 Something must be really wrong with women, as even asexual beings have a problem with them ☺
13 It is like telling your first-born, that from today onwards, (s)he will have to accept that the parents' hearts equally love a sibling, who was not, and is now.

love God as the most unbearable suffering of all sufferings. His ultra-rabid reaction to his impotency is to torture all fallen creatures. This way the satan supplies to their suffering, what their less developed understanding of not seeing God, still lacks.[14]

This summarizes the consistency of there being evil in a world, created by an Infinitely Good Being: everything follows from the concept of a "created, whence imperfect freedom".[15] However, having a theologically consistent understanding of oneself and of God, is by no means necessary to access to Heaven. Whores will "precede" the

---

14 For my dear non-believing readership: this is orders of magnitude worse than Hannibal the Cannibal
15 Later Catholic epigones, like Calvin, got this teaching all wrong, whence they introduced their "double predestination". This term graphically meant that the names of the elect and the damned were written down in two books, whence the term "double". Why is this inconsistent? Well, because determination in God's Mind, is nothing but overseeing beginning and end of Creation, or if you wish, it is the necessary consequence of God's power to confer freedom to its creatures. How could the Creator of freedom not know how that freedom is going to be used? The incomprehensibility of this perfectly understandable consistence is hidden in the fact that God's actively knowing what a creature is going to do, does not determine in a human, classical sense what that person is going to do. Who fails to understand this, becomes by definition an inconsistent believer in double predestination. It is inconsistent, because it declares human freedom a fake, while, on the other hand, Jesus left no doubt as to the reality of human freedom. He "had no choice", because an infinitely just God can under no reasonable pretense damn a being that never had an opportunity to choose in the first place.

Pharisees,[16] even if they cannot spell their own name. Therefore, whatever belief the reader might adhere to, I urge you to stay put in your creed, and bear with me a little more, whether I consider your belief inconsistent or not.

By now the reader should be able to understand, within the Catholic framework, the difference between satanic and non-satanic child abuse. Non-satanic child abuse is primarily due to lust for having sex with children. The risk categories are well documented and catalogued: number one (by far) being the second boyfriend of a mother with a young girl from an earlier marriage. Number two are male sport teachers, number three the male youth club leaders. Homosexuality is a severe risk category for pedophilia, however strongly gays pretend the opposite. Females only exceptionally abuse of children: when ordered so by charismatic males, or when integrated in male-controlled satanic cults. It is too bad the Catholic Church has been and still is involved in child abuse. In my view, this is mainly due to the Bergoglio's,[17]

---

16 Here, the verb "precede" is meant ironically: all Pharisees who definitely chose against Jesus do not enter Heaven; whatever Saint (immediately!) John Paul the Great might have argued against it. Especially, Jesus' words that "it was better for Judas not to have born", leave no room for free interpretation.
17 [https://www.youtube.com/watch?v=OFtTHKRO6-k] In 2011 Cardinal Carlo Viganò wrote a letter to Pope Benedict XVI concerning Cardinal McCarrick's repeated child abuses, bluntly calling him a "serial predator". As a consequence, Pope Benedict XVI immediately defrocked McCarrick. When Bergoglio

Satanic Child Abuse

the Paglia's, the Danneels' and his mafia, whose pedophilia turns them into a prime risk category of child abuse. The sooner Catholics get rid of such hell-steering monsters, the sooner priestly child abuse will be reduced to a dead relict of the 1960 decade of "sexual revolution".

While non-satanic child abuse is typified by the perpetrator's deep longing for sexual intercourse with young meat, satanic child abuse contains no such longing at all: it is the intellectual endeavor to please the satan in return for his help in matters of earthly power. Evidently, all people who are mentally sane and do things like that, necessarily must be followers of Manus, as that is the typical creed that gives evil 50% odds of defeating good.

Well, my dear reader, if you survived this brutal introduction, you have an enhanced chance of surviving the rest of this book, too. No guarantee, however, because things get really ugly.

Here is but a little example of how the Holy See actually tries to introduce pedophilia into the One, Holy, and Catholic Church. I leave the full quote in Spanish:[18]

---

usurped the throne, he immediately reinstated McCarrick, in spite of Viganò's personal warning letters. Another "heroic" action taken by Bergoglio, immediately after succeeding Pope Benedict XVI, is finishing with the latter's tribunal for dirty Bishops.

18 http://www.ewtnnoticias.com/noticias-catolicas/noticia.php?id=34338

Una llamada telefónica que podría pasar a la historia del cine. El pasado martes por la noche, el Papa Francisco habría llamado Roberto Benigni, escritor, director y protagonista de la película italiana ganadora del Oscar "La vida es bella", para hablar sobre los Diez Mandamientos. El director y actor toscano, llevó recientemente a la televisión italiana unas reflexiones religiosas, morales y civiles sobre "Los Diez Mandamientos", que fueron seguidas durante dos noches consecutivas por nueve millones de espectadores el primer día, y diez el segundo. Aunque la Oficina de Prensa de la Santa Sede no ha confirmado la llamada del Papa, en declaraciones a la revista italiana Famiglia Cristiana, el Presidente del Pontificio Consejo para la Familia, Arzobispo Vincenzo Paglia, afirma que "no me sorprende nada que el Papa Francisco haya llamado a Roberto Benigni". Mons. Paglia también telefoneó al director toscano después del éxito televisivo del programa, emitido el 15 y el 16 de diciembre en el canal italiano Rai Uno. "No me dijo el contenido la llamada, pero me lo puedo imaginar (risas). Roberto estaba muy sorprendido por este boom de oyentes, el increíble aumento de audiencia desde el primer día, 'ha sido algo

Satanic Child Abuse xiii

> extraordinario, incluso milagroso', me subrayó. Le he escuchado bastante conmovido, incluso me dijo que la gente lo para por la calle, y hasta alguno le ha pedido bromeando ¡que le bautice a sus hijos!", señaló Mons. Paglia. "Su transmisión sobre los Diez Mandamientos encaja bien en el cauce de la Iglesia en salida, querida por Bergoglio. En este caso, se trata de un artista en salida que sabe usar el bagaje de la sabiduría sin muchos ornamentos. Y no es casualidad que el Papa, en su exhortación apostólica *Evangelii Gaudium* dedicara un espacio enorme al tema de la predicación, haciendo de su homilía matutina en Santa Marta su magisterio habitual", añadió la autoridad vaticana. Aunque el director de cine no se declara creyente, en 2008 participó en una maratón televisiva ininterrumpida para leer la Biblia. El evento involucró 1.200 personas durante seis días, y fue iniciado con la lectura del Génesis por el mismo Papa Benedicto XVI.

For those who do not read Spanish: Monsignor Vincenzo Paglia, Chamberlain of the Pope, is a pedophile himself, and was invited by the Pope to publicize homosexuality as "another option" of living the Divine call. It suffices to read the Jewish Bible (the Catholic "Old Testament") to realize that this will never ever going to happen to Catholicism, no matter how many Bergoglio's it shall have to suffer.

CHAPTER 1

History

1.1 Ancient Cultures

I guess there is no history without satanic child abuse. Wherever one looks, one finds it. Aztecs, for one, were very good at it. We should be collectively grateful to the great Mel Gibson for only having shown us a mere glimpse of what Aztec High Priests did to adults from subjected tribes, without plunging into the full filth of children sacrifices. They tore out their victims' hearts in order to offer these, still beating, to satan, the "owner of the sun and of all life". From the Old Testament one infers that Ancient Semites had the same problem, obviously copy-pasted from neighboring cultures, like the Ancient Egyptian, the Ancient Assyrian, and the Ancient Persian.

No doubt Noah's flooding was merely meant to wipe out all cultures that ritually offered children to satan, in much the same way as the two cities of Sodom and

Gomorra were wiped out for their aggressively assaulting homosexuality, whence pedophilia and child abuse.[19]

Many Christians have a hard time understanding all the blood shed in the Old Testament. It is very simple: either you violently fight against satanic children offerings, or the satan swallows you. Hence, whenever God gives his elected the order *to fully wipe out a tribe, and annihilate all booty*, that is not for the mere pleasure of seeing people die. God only orders direct killing when such is the only means to keep society at a minimum of supernatural health. This is the only and enough reason for God to immediately dethrone Saul after his faked annihilation of the Amalekite culture.

So when did satanic child abuse enter human history? Well, at the very beginning: Shortly after Adam and Eve's original sin. The consequence of that sin, for Adam and Eve, was their immediate expulsion from the garden of Eden. Too bad, original sin had consequences for their progeny, too. With regard to the progeny, however, it is an error to think of original sin as an actual sin perpetrated by the progeny, however many Canonized Church Fathers seem to believe this. For the progeny, original sin is nothing but *a condition of human nature, consisting*

---

[19] The prude Bible text only mentions Lot's adult daughter, but sometimes one has to read between the lines. Do you really think a mob of angry homosexuals would accept a single virgin to satisfy their needs?

History 3

(among many others) in a reduced self-control with respect to that of Adam and Eve before their fall. The Old Testament describes this elegantly and visually by Adam and Eve's hiding their nakedness. This is not meant literally. It is meant spiritually: before the fall, both Adam and Eve so much mastered their lust, that they had no problem in curbing their sexual desires according to reason. No matter if they walked around naked or fully clothed. That is just the image. Reality is, that after the fall, they did not master their desires any more, whether sexual or not. Hence they behaved like very annoyed, short of confessing to one another that they had turned into slaves of their desire. Well, exactly that, their having turned into slaves of their desires, is the destiny of all their progeny.

So thank you, Adam and Eve, there we are, slaves of our desires. The only reason the Church shows gratitude towards you, is that God could not bear the sight of all your progeny ending up in hell. Your sin was the opportunity God freely took, in order to save us from that bondage.

1.2 Modern Cultures

After the "failed divine efforts" to mold the Jews into his elected people, God announced "in his wrath" that election would befall the heathens. The Sadducees so much disliked this prophecy, that they threw out all Prophets, Psalms and Wisom from the Jewish Bible, reducing it to the Pentateuch, the first five books. Their names in Ancient Hebrew, English, and Greek are

- Bəreshit (בְּרֵאשִׁית, literally "In the beginning") — **Genesis**, from Γένεσις (Génesis, "Creation")
- Shəmot (מוֹת, literally "Names") — **Exodus**, from Ἔξοδος (Éxodos, "Exit")
- Vayikra (יִּקְרָא, literally "And He called") — **Leviticus**, from Λευιτικόν (Leuitikón, "Relating to the Levites")
- Bəmidbar (מִדְבַּר, literally "In the desert [of]") — **Numbers**, from Ἀριθμοί (Arithmoí, "Numbers")
- Dəvarim (בָּרִים, literally "Things" or "Words") — **Deuteronomy**, from Δευτερονόμιον (Deuteronómion, "Second-Law")

History   5

These are the books that contain the well-known quote "I am the God worshiped by Abraham, Isaac, and Jacob",[20] which Jesus used to ridicule the Sadducees' inconsistent conception of resurrection. Sadducees were already quite angered by all of God's prophets, who kept rebuking them, and now comes the Son Himself, and He even pokes fun at the highest Priestly and Civil Authorities! I find it very understandable that the Sadducees went completely out of their minds: In their place, possibly I would have done the same thing, too. *Are we*, who studied the Scriptures through thousands of years, to be taught "the truth" by some "nouveau-poor" carpenter from a dispersed non-Judaic village in the illiterate heathen north of Israel?

---

20 [Mt 22, 23-32]: The Sadducees did not believe that people would rise to life after death. So that same day some of the Sadducees came to Jesus and said: Teacher, Moses wrote that if a married man dies and has no children, his brother should marry the widow. Their first son would then be thought of as the son of the dead brother. Once there were seven brothers who lived here. The first one married, but died without having any children. So his wife was left to his brother. The same thing happened to the second and third brothers and finally to all seven of them. At last the woman died. When God raises people from death, whose wife will this woman be? She had been married to all seven brothers. Jesus answered: "You are completely wrong! You don't know what the Scriptures teach. And you don't know anything about the power of God. When God raises people to life, they won't marry. They will be like the angels in heaven. And as for people being raised to life, God was speaking to you when he said, 'I am the God worshiped by Abraham, Isaac, and Jacob'. He isn't the God of the dead, but of the living."

Jesus' destiny was quickly settled: he made it no further than his 33rd. The Sadducees had wrung his death penalty through the throat of local representative of the Romman power, "what-is-truth" Pilate. The latter would later witness his mini-empire falling into pieces, his wife turning away from him in profound disgust, and worst of all, her becoming a member of that appalling "Christian Sect".

The fall of Jerusalem AD 70 finished with Salomon's Temple; if we may believe the prophecy, for once and for all. Little is known of what became of the Pharisees. Many of them converted to Christianity, and many more kept a fond remembrance of that unique and courageous prophet, who silenced the Sadducees in their stupid refusal of the existence of angels, and in rejeccting the plain historical fact of His Own resurrection.

St. Paul would later, when forced to by his accusers, shrewdly play out Sadducees against Pharisees in their bipartite Congress. On the other hand, Sadducees kept confabulating, first in their synagogues, and later in their private houses, planning the longest-term reconquest that I could ever have imagined.[21] That is how the "divinely elected, pure Jewish bloodlines" started their ultra-racist mafia, which today happens to be led by Jacob Rothschild.

---

21 This is, in itself, a quite clear sign of demonic possession

History

They were not particularly fond of child abuse. For them, it was a necessary evil to obtain satan's help to realize their long-term reconquest: To subdue all heathens into slavery of god's elected people. Since they would never even think of offering their own children to the satan, they were always in need of other people's children, *whether Jewish or not*.

Of course, antidefamation leagues consider me an anti-Semite. Wrong: *I love all righteous Semites,* be they Hebrews, Palestinians, Arabs or whatever other subsubusubsubspecies of humanity. Evil is always caused by a very tiny fraction of a country's people. So no anti-Semitism here: Only hard feelings toward mafias and their puppets. No racism either: I am not a Semite, yet I love them. End of argument.

The most consistent racists I have ever met are the very Jewish members of the Sadducee mafia. In comparison, the German Aryans following a genetic Jew called Hitler, is but a satire of consistency. A satire like Dante's Comedy.

Whatever some elect Jews might have *interpreted,* it is simply impossible, on the basis of the full Jewish Bible (law, prophets, and wisdom), to be a racist, unless one expressly discards all passages about foreigners. Let me name but two among the very many.

Zarephath (Heb. צָרְפַת) was a Phoenician city, economically and politically dependent of Sidon. God commanded his prophet Elijah the Tishbite to go to this city, during the great drought in the reign of Ahab. There he met a widow whom he nourished miraculously, throughout the barren period, because of her faith manifested by her unimaginable offer *in extremis*.[22]

When somewhat later the widow's only son died, Elijah revived him, after having rebuked God. In the second book of Kings we meet Elijah once again, cleansing Syrian military commander-in-chief Naaman from his leprosy.[23] The episode turned out fatally for Elijah's

---

22 [1 Kings 17, 11-14] And as she was going to fetch water, he called to her, and said: Bring me, I pray thee, a morsel of bread in thine hand. And she said, As the Lord thy God liveth, I have not a cake, but a handful of meal in a barrel, and a little oil in a cruse: and, behold, I am gathering two sticks, that I may go in and dress it for me and my son, that we may eat it, and die. And Elijah said unto her, Fear not; go and do as thou hast said: but make me thereof a little cake first, and bring it unto me, and after make for thee and for thy son. For thus saith the Lord God of Israel: The barrel of meal shall not waste, neither shall the cruse of oil fail, until the day that the Lord sendeth rain upon the earth.
23 [2 Kings 5, 1-27] Naaman was the commander of the Syrian army. The Lord had helped him and his troops defeat their enemies, so the king of Syria respected Naaman very much. Naaman was a brave soldier, but he had leprosy. One day while the Syrian troops were raiding Israel, they captured a girl, and she became a servant of Naaman's wife. Sometime later the girl said, "If your husband Naaman would go to the prophet in Samaria, he would be cured of his leprosy." When Naaman told the king what the girl had said, the king replied, "Go ahead! I will give you a letter to take to the king of Israel." Naaman left and took along seven hundred fifty pounds of silver, one hundred fifty pounds of gold, and ten new outfits. He also carried the letter to the king of Israel. It said, "I am sending my

History

servant Naaman to you. Would you cure him of his leprosy?" When the king of Israel read the letter, he tore his clothes in fear and shouted, "That Syrian king believes I can cure this man of leprosy! Does he think I'm God with power over life and death? He must be trying to pick a fight with me." As soon as Elisha the prophet heard what had happened, he sent the Israelite king this message: "Why are you so afraid? Send the man to me, so that he will know there is a prophet in Israel." Naaman left with his horses and chariots and stopped at the door of Elisha's house. Elisha sent someone outside to say to him, "Go wash seven times in the Jordan River. Then you'll be completely cured." But Naaman stormed off, grumbling, "Why couldn't he come out and talk to me? I thought for sure he would stand in front of me and pray to the Lord his God, then wave his hand over my skin and cure me. What about the Abana River or the Pharpar River? Those rivers in Damascus are just as good as any river in Israel. I could have washed in them and been cured." His servants went over to him and said, "Sir, if the prophet had told you to do something difficult, you would have done it. So why don't you do what he said? Go wash and be cured." Naaman walked down to the Jordan; he waded out into the water and stooped down in it seven times, just as Elisha had told him. Right away, he was cured, and his skin became as smooth as a child's. Naaman and his officials went back to Elisha. Naaman stood in front of him and announced, "Now I know that the God of Israel is the only God in the whole world. Sir, would you please accept a gift from me?" "I am a servant of the living Lord," Elisha answered, "and I swear that I will not take anything from you." Naaman kept begging, but Elisha kept refusing. Finally Naaman said, "If you won't accept a gift, then please let me take home as much soil as two mules can pull in a wagon. Sir, from now on I will offer sacrifices only to the Lord. But I pray that the Lord will forgive me when I go into the temple of the god Rimmon and bow down there with the king of Syria." "Go on home, and don't worry about that," Elisha replied. Then Naaman left. After Naaman had gone only a short distance, Gehazi said to himself, "Elisha let that Syrian off too easy. He should have taken Naaman's gift. I swear by the living Lord that I will talk to Naaman myself and get something from him." So he hurried after Naaman. When Naaman saw Gehazi servant Gehazi. He ended up a leper, with the Divine curse extending over his progeny until extinction.

Not only Jews, in great numbers, are unable to correctly interpret such Old-Testament passages: Christians fail so, too. Some of the latter are foolishly proud of their *pacifism,* presently backed up by Pope Jorge Mario Bergoglio in this respect. Some even claim that pacifism distinguishes the Old from the New Testament.

Modicae Fidei! Why did the Christ tell us he was bringing the sword, setting up family members one against the other? Why did God wish that Peter baptize

---

running after him, he got out of his chariot to meet him. Naaman asked, "Is everything all right?" "Yes," Gehazi answered. "But my master has sent me to tell you about two young prophets from the hills of Ephraim. They came asking for help, and now Elisha wants to know if you would give them about seventy-five pounds of silver and some new clothes?" "Sure," Naaman replied. "But why don't you take twice that amount of silver?" He convinced Gehazi to take it all, then put the silver in two bags. He handed the bags and the clothes to his two servants, and they carried them for Gehazi. When they reached the hill where Gehazi lived, he took the bags from the servants and placed them in his house, then sent the men away. After they had gone, Gehazi went in and stood in front of Elisha, who asked, "Gehazi, where have you been?" "Nowhere, sir," Gehazi answered. Elisha asked, "Don't you know that my spirit was there when Naaman got out of his chariot to talk with you? Gehazi, you have no right to accept money or clothes, olive orchards or vineyards, sheep or cattle, or servants. Because of what you've done, Naaman's leprosy will now be on you and your descendants forever!" Suddenly, Gehazi's skin became white with leprosy, and he left.

and *confirm*[24] Cornelius, Captain of the "Italian Unit"?[25] Why would Jesus praise a *Roman Army Officer for a faith not found in the whole of Israel?*.[26]

That means, my dear pacifist Christians, that Jesus considers faith much more important than anything else, and moreover, *that being an army officer in an occupying foreign power includes not the least trace of sin*. This also holds for Naaman's praying with his King to a fictional god. Hence, with the Christian Scriptures in one's hand, it is even more difficult to be a racist. I feel deeply intertwined with all people on earth, simply

---

24 Confirmation is a Catholic Sacrament instituted by the Christ on Pentecost, which completes the grace received in baptism.
25 Acts 10,1
26 [Luke 7, 1-10] After Jesus had finished teaching the people, he went to Capernaum. In that town an army officer's servant was sick and about to die. The officer liked this servant very much. And when he heard about Jesus, he sent some Jewish leaders to ask him to come and heal the servant. The leaders went to Jesus and begged him to do something. They said, "This man deserves your help! He loves our nation and even built us a meeting place." So Jesus went with them. When Jesus wasn't far from the house, the officer sent some friends to tell him, "Lord, don't go to any trouble for me! I am not good enough for you to come into my house. And I am certainly not worthy to come to you. Just say the word, and my servant will get well. I have officers who give orders to me, and I have soldiers who take orders from me. I can say to one of them, 'Go!' and he goes. I can say to another, 'Come!' and he comes. I can say to my servant, 'Do this!' and he will do it." When Jesus heard this, he was so surprised that he turned and said to the crowd following him, "In all of Israel I've never found anyone with this much faith!" The officer's friends returned and found the servant well.

because every human is, just like me, a free creature made by a perfect God. And "meat is of no use", as Christians shoud know better than anybody else: Only spirit matters.

Returning to our core business (the above-mentioned child offerings), they were indeed common practice among the Jewish Sadducees, although not at all a uniquely Jewish practice, as it was common to *all possible* ancient cultures. Think, for example, of the historically well-documented Aztecs and their rites (quite well represented by genius Mel Gibson).[27]

These are three completely different things. And be rather sure about it, that if Islamic or Christian children were not readily available on the market, Sadducees would just as easily fish for victims among non-Sadducee Jews. We saw exactly the same happen in World War II: the Sadducee mafia needed a lot of money, and stole all German-Jewish money by having a dictator puppet killing them. Jewish savings, already deposited in Sadducee banks,[28] were just *waiting for some morally acceptable reason to get away with all of it.*

Since after World War II there were no German Jews left to claim their savings, the Sadducees had it their way. That many Jews died? Collateral damage. Sorry guys, this

---

[27] whence vomited out by the Sadducee Hollywood & FED & media mafia
[28] ordinary Jews would never think of saving their money in heathens' banks

History 13

is business as usual, no personal grudge here. If people die, it is not because the Sadducees *dislike nor despize them*, but because they are but standing in the way.

In the specific case of World War II, there was an additional business advantage. The German Christians could later be fully wrung by claiming compensation for German-Jewish financial and moral losses, a business move called "Wiedergutmachung", which the Germans would be too stupid to understand.[29] German Christians were collectively ingenuous enough to keep paying the very perpetrators of WW II, and what is much worse, they would eventually fall into a collective guilt syndrome.

Had this not been a traumatic experience for the huge majority of innocent Germans, of Jewish and Aryan genotype alike,[30] it would have been a jaw-breaking joke.

---

[29] The German word for compensation. Literally: the "make it up" to former victims.

[30] Why were the German Jews so rich? Because like in no other country in Europe, Germans of autochtonous pedigree knew how to fraternize with Germans of Jewish pedigree, in spite of the latter consistently refusing to mix genetically with the autochtonous Germans.

1.3 Freemasonries

During the Middle Ages ornamental masons grouped together, laying the bases of the later guilds. The earliest official documents referring to masons are written in Latin or Norman French. Thus we have "sculptores lapidum liberorum" (London 1212), "magister lathomus liberarum petrarum" (Oxford 1391), and "mestre mason de franche peer" (Statute of Labourers 1351). These all signify a worker in freestone, a grainless sandstone or limestone suitable for ornamental masonry.

In the 17th century building accounts of Wadham College the terms freemason and freestone mason are used interchangeably.[31] Hence the term "free" does not stem from "freedom" but from "freestone".

The original use of the word "lodge" indicates a workshop erected on the site of a major work, the first mention being Vale Royal Abbey in 1278. Later, it gained the secondary meaning of the community of masons in a particular place. It took five full centuries for the lodges to evolve, from mere craftsmen guild, into secret societies with heavily perverted goals.

---

[31] https://en.wikipedia.org/wiki/History_of_Freemasonry

History

The 18th century John Theophilus Desaguliers, a French-born British clergyman, is often described as the "father" of modern freemasonry and so-called Grand-Lodges. Although he only served one term as Grand Master, he was twice Deputy Grand Master under figurehead Grand Masters, and at other times behaved as if he was Grand Master, forming irregular lodges to conduct secret initiations.

The oldest Irish records indicate that Royal Arch Chapters originally administered three degrees. The first was based on the refurbishment of the first temple by the Ancient Jewish King Josiah. The second was a short bridge to the third, which was based on the rebuilding of the temple after the exile.

In the wake of the French Revolution, the British Government became uneasy about possible revolutionary conspiracies. Amongst other repressive measures, Pitt's government proposed to introduce the Unlawful Societies Act in 1799, which declared that any political body which administered a secret oath was illegal. Acting quickly, a delegation representing the Ancients, Moderns and the Grand Lodge of Scotland arranged a meeting with the Prime Minister. The delegation included the Duke of Atholl, Grand Master of the Ancients, and Past Grand Master Mason of the Grand Lodge of Scotland, and the Earl of Moira, Acting Grand Master of the Moderns (the Grand Master being the Prince of Wales). As a result of this meeting, Freemasons were specifically excluded from the act, although lodges were obliged to return a list of members to the local Clerk of the Peace, a practice which continued until 1967.

In the US, the Grand Lodges prospered, too, except during a period marked by the murder of William Morgan (1826) in Batavia, New York, after his threatening to expose Freemasonic secrets. Benjamin Franklin re-issued Anderson's 1723 constitutions as Provincial Grand Master of Pennsylvania. George Washington was initiated into the Lodge of Fredericksburg in 1752.[32]

Theodore Zeldin writes the following about 19th century French freemasonry:[33]

> Freemasonry appealed first of all to people who liked mystic ritual, esoteric symbolism and fancy uniforms, and to those who like to have somewhere to discuss ideas and meet like-minded friends. Increasingly however it became an organization which politicians used for electoral purposes in which civil servants joined in order to further their chances of promotion, which hotel-keepers found useful as a way of enlarging their clientele and where

---

[32] http://freemasonry.bcy.ca/biography/washington_g/washington_g.html
[33] Zeldin, France 1848–1945 (1977) 2:1032–33

History

businessmen could make deals and find jobs for their sons.

He fails to mention, though, that the 19th century French freemasonry became increasingly anti-Catholic, and the Catholic Church increasingly anti-masonic. Obviously not because the Church's doctrine changed, but because that of the freemasons changed. Their increasing greed was a highway for hell's angel motorbike to ride in. Of course, he took ten worse colleagues with him, to celebrate the party. The worst of them was satan himself, who always requires child offers.

1.4 Freemasonic American Presidents

Not all freemasons are bad people, though. Below the highest achievable women's "degree", freemasonry is nothing but a humanitarian window dressing for what happens in the superior, exclusively male levels, to wit, secret dealings with devils. The "honor" to deal with satan himself is exclusive to the highest, or 33rd, degree.

History

President	Cult
George Washington (1732–1799)	Worshipful Master 1788 Fredericksburgh Lodge, Virginia
James Monroe (1758–1831)	Initiated 1775 Williamsburg Lodge, Virginia
Andrew Jackson (1767–1845)	Grand Master 1822 Nashville Lodge Tennessee
James K. Polk (1795–1849)	Initiated 1820 Columbia Lodge, Tennessee
James Buchanan (1791–1868)	District Deputy Grand Master 1824 Lancaster and York
Andrew Johnson (1808–1875)	Initiated 1851 Greenville Lodge, Tennessee
James A. Garfield (1831–1881)	Chaplain 1868 of Columbus Lodge, Ohio
William McKinley (1843–1901)	Charter member of 1867 Eagle (Canton) Lodge, Ohio
Theodore Roosevelt (1858–1919)	Initiated 1901 Oyster Bay Lodge, New York
William H. Taft (1857–1930)	Initiated 1909 Kilwinning Lodge, Cincinnati, Ohio
Warren G. Harding (1865–1923)	Initiated 1901 Marion Lodge, Ohio
Franklin D. Roosevelt (1882–1945)	Grand Master 1934 New York Order
Harry S. Truman (1884–1972)	Grand Master 1911 Grandview Lodge, Missouri
Gerald Ford (1913–2006)	Grand Master 1962 Columbia Lodge, Washington, D.C.

Many US presidents were freemasons, as shown by the table above.³⁴ Be aware of humanitarian institutes!³⁵ While James Garfield was a post-restoration Church-of-Christ cleric, chaplain of his lodge, and an upright Christian, in the 20th century the lodges turned on average, from merely anti-Catholic, to anti-Christian, thereby merely reflecting the general trend observed outside the lodges.

He had an ultra-short term of but half a year, for being shot by one of Conkling's stalwarts. The horrible medical treatment he received after the non-fatal shot wounds are a clear sign of conspiracy. Like Abraham Lincoln, James Garfield left little doubt concerning his printing greenbacks, according to blogger FSK (January 24, 2010):³⁶

> James Garfield knew that the financial industry was one big scam. Even in 1881 before the creation of the Federal Reserve, a regulated financial industry was forced to operate under corrupt fractional reserve principles. (...) James Garfield was planning to

---

34 https://en.wikipedia.org/wiki/List_of_Presidents_of_the _United_States_who_were_Freemasons
35 A spectacular one is the putrid Clinton Foundation
36 http://fskrealityguide.blogspot.com/2010/01/did-banksters-kill-james-garfield.html

History

issue more Greenbacks, like President Lincoln did to finance the Civil War. The bankers are very hostile to credit-based fiat money directly spent into circulation by the government. Such money does not come with debt-strings attached, and helps people escape the chains of debt slavery. In the present, deficit spending is financed by Treasury Bonds, which are owned by the bankers. The only reason the Federal government doesn't directly spend money into circulation is that contradicts the interests of the bankers. Even though the banking cartel has a lot of power, they sometimes make a mistake and let someone with a clue become President. James Garfield is an example of such an error. Such mistakes are easily corrected via an assassination. That both eliminates a threat and sends a message to all other politicians, making sure they don't behave too honestly. There's another interesting thing about these "Presidents were assassinated!" conspiracy theories. Lincoln, Garfield, and Kennedy were all hostile to the interests of the bankers, and all three were assassinated. For each of them, the official State explanation was "It was a lone crazy person responsible for the assassination!" rather than "Insiders killed him to protect their interests!" (...) Some people say that the Secret Service that protects the President is really good. The President could not be assassinated unless his security team allowed it. (...) some Secret Service agents were also on the payroll of the bankers. The Secret Service doesn't just protect the President. The Secret Service also spies on the President all the time. The Secret Service helps make sure that the President isn't exposed to any "dangerous" ideas. If you're one of the insiders working for the banking cartel, it isn't too hard to hire someone to conduct an assassination, and then deny any connection to the bankers.

History

Freemasons have some very childish behaviors. I remember I did those things in my tender youth: communicating with my friends using secret signs. Here is Andrew Jackson in full freemason pose. He did not understand that freemasonry automatically implies financial fraud, and paid for it with his life.

Due to their protestant background, freemasons in general, and freemasonic presidents in special, were a relatively easy prey for the Sadducee mafia. This is not so much due to the Protestant creed, but to the historical fact that Protestantism had always been impregnated with an absolute submission to their divinely appointed Kings or Queens, while Catholics, frequently absurdly ill-treated by them,[37] looked for spiritual salvation to God and Rome.

---

[37] Catholic suffering and torture under Anglicanism, Calvinism,

They were by definition considered as potential defectors or spies in war times "because of their allegiance to a foreign sovereign nation". Protestant leaders were time and again utterly unable to understand Christ's prescription "give to the Caesar what is Caesar's, and to God what is God's." Alternatively, they had "omitted" to evaluate the military reach and endeavors of the modern Vatican.[38]

Long after and quite oppite to the righteous Andrew Jackson, the also freemasonic President Franklin Delano Roosevelt was a total disaster for the US citizens, and a blessing for the Sadducee mafia.[39] He had a profound disregard for law, as he was convinced to be a the best dictator ever happened to the US. As such, he is well known for his appalling butchery in Haiti, his self-

---

and Lutheranism is extremely disgusting, and of a scale utterly incomparable to what the French Huguenots suffered under the hands of a Catholic King. This is all consistently silenced in protestant history books.

38 It does have a Pontifical Swiss Guard, though. It is one of the oldest military units (1506) in the world. It is also the smallest army in the world (136 soldiers). They are armed with halberds, the blade of which carried the Royal arms in gold, as well as gold-hilted swords. To data, they carry modern arms as well. However, they are not even able to defend the Vatican against drone attacks.

39 http://www.whatreallyhappened.com/WRHARTICLES/pearl/
www.geocities.com/Pentagon/6315/fdr.html

confessed felony,[40] and his equally appalling butchery of homosexuals.[41]

---

40 Cook, pp 265-266: 1 February 1920 before an audience of 1500 at the Brooklyn Academy of Music, FDR said, "Two months after the war was declared, I saw that the Navy was still unprepared and I spent $40,000 for guns before Congress gave me or anyone permission to spend the money." This action had been opposed by the President. FDR further boasted that he had "committed enough illegal acts" to be impeached and jailed for "999 years"

41 A Senate subcommittee concluded that FDR had committed perjury before a Naval Court of Inquiry about his investigation of a homosexual corruption ring at the Newport, RI, Naval Station. FDR, as Assistant Secretary of the Navy, had approved the use of decoys to entrap homosexuals (young sailors were instructed in and ordered by FDR's men to perform homosexual acts and the details truly are unprintable). When it became an issue he had lied about it to the Court. He had signed an order for investigators to go "to the limit" but he denied under oath that he had read what he had signed and swore he had no idea what was in the order. On June 11, 1919, FDR had personally taken charge of every aspect of the case, the most extensive systematic persecution of homosexual men in American history. When the facts emerged FDR denied he knew anything about it and if he had known about it he said he would have stopped it. FDR's testimony under oath at the May 1920 Navy Board of Inquiry was the height of arrogance. How did he suppose evidence for sodomy could be obtained, he was asked. FDR:"As a lawyer, I had no idea. That is not within the average lawyer's education." Did you realize as a lawyer or a man of intelligence that the investigation of such matters, very often has led to improper actions? FDR:"I never had such an idea. Never entered my head..." How did you think evidence of these things could be obtained? FDR:"I didn't think. If I had thought, I would have supposed they had someone under the bed or looking over the transom." (Cook pp 267-271 and Ward pp 488-490) The Senate subcommittee also found "Roosevelt's actions displayed an utter lack of moral perspective." (Ward pp 571-572)

As far as the New Deal is concerned, we refer to Garet Garrett's "The People's Pottage: The Revolution Was", and to Al Smith's speech "The Facts in the Case" given January 25, 1936, to the American Liberty League. For his New Deal, FDR is often considered a Communist. This is exactly what the Sadducee mafia was desperately trying to achieve in Russia.

FDR was infuriated in May 1941 by Hitler' decision to transfer the Luftwaffe to the eastern Front. FDR was so distraught that he not only totally lost control of his emotions but also control of his body functions- he was bedridden for a month. FDR declared a national emergency and put the country on a war footing. In May, he ordered a 25,000 man Expeditionary Force to be ready to fight anywhere on June 22 - the date he knew Russia was to be invaded! FDR said: "My own thought is that perhaps there is one word that we could use for this war. The word *Survival*. The Survival War." The only country fighting for survival was the Soviet Union. Only FDR wanted it to survive.

Churchill came away from the Atlantic Conference on August 14, 1941, observing the "astonishing depth of Roosevelt's intense desire for war."

FDR, who had always reacted to stress with illness, was so stressed that his immune system malfunctioned and he immediately contracted polio on the publication of the Senate report.

Before we entered the war, FDR sent a delegation to the Vatican to get the Pope to endorse communism – the Pope refused. With lend-lease, a.k.a. Lenin-lease, before Pearl Harbor, FDR pressed his aides to allocate and speed shipments to the Soviet Union in the strongest possible way.

FDR exerted frenetic personal devotion to the cause of lend-lease to the communists, distinctly favoring Russia over Britain (and US) and if you read page 549 volume 3 of The Secret Diaries of Harold Ickes, Ickes makes it clear that in a choice between England and Russia FDR would have abandoned England: "if the (public) attitude had been one of angry suspicion or even resentment, we would have been confronted with the alternative of abandoning Great Britain or accepting communism..." On August 1, 1941 FDR said about planes for Russia, "we must get 'em, even if it necessary to take from our own troops." Ickes said "we ought to come pretty close to stripping ourselves in view of Russian aid." The US sent 150 P-40's (the newest) when we were woefully short. In 1944 Churchill publicly complained about Britain being treated worse than the Soviet Union (in 1943 we sent 5,000 planes to Russia; overall we sent 20,000 planes and 400,000 trucks - twice as many as they had had before the war, 9 million pairs of boots, complete factories as part of $11 billion in aid that was never expected to be paid back). FDR's oil embargo of Japan forcing them South to take oil-rich Dutch Indonesia, is incomprehensible unless you realize FDR did it to relieve Japanese military threats to the Soviet Union.

FDR broke all commitments that he had made — not to go to war, the 4 freedoms, the Atlantic Charter and limitlessly misrepresented his foreign policies and his commitments at Yalta both publicly and privately.

A problem for mythmakers is that if Pearl Harbor was a surprise to FDR, then he was a victim, not a maker of history; he did not lead the nation into war for reasons of world morality but was forced into it or drawn into it or compelled to take up arms against his will, by circumstances beyond his control. If Pearl Harbor was not a surprise, FDR was a traitor. Obviously, he was a traitor to his own soldiers in Pearl Harbor, whose orders were to maximize the number of casualties. This would gather him the sufficient number of free subscriptions to the US invasion army.

In August 2009 Rafael Medoff (director of The David S. Wyman Institute for Holocaust Studies) writes a book

History

commentary in Haaretz[42] entitled "Israel History / Would the Real Harry Truman Please Stand Up?" The book, "A Safe Haven: Harry S Truman and the Founding of Israel" (HarperCollins), is written by Allis Radosh and Ronald Radosh.

Would the Real Harry Truman Please Stand Up? Rhadosh' bothers' book questions Truman's integrity and founding role of Israel as a Safe Haven for 100,000 Jews.

An examination of the 33rd president's motives in recognizing Israel may leave the reader puzzled. Did Truman feel any real support for Zionism, or was he just fishing for the votes of American Jews?

President Harry Truman's recognition of the newborn State of Israel, on May 14, 1948, was greeted by American Jewish leaders with a torrent of adulatory telegrams and press releases. One congressman, however, added a

---

42 https://www.haaretz.com/israel-news/culture/1.5087382

dissenting note. "President Truman is entitled to fulsome praise for his example of statesmanship in recognizing the State of Israel," Emanuel Celler, Democrat of Brooklyn, announced. "It is now essential for the United States to go the full way ... The ridiculous [U.S.] arms embargo should now be lifted for the benefit of the State of Israel ... " The stark contrast between Truman's on-paper recognition of the state and the reality of Israel fighting, without tanks, artillery or armored vehicles, against five invading Arab armies dramatizes the complex task faced by historians in assessing Truman's role in the state's creation and survival. Did Truman recognize Israel out of sincere support for Zionism, or merely in order to secure Jewish votes in that November's presidential election? Why did the president overrule the State Department on the recognition issue, but not on the arms embargo? If Truman was sincerely committed to Israel's survival, how could he refuse to give it arms for self-defense?

In "A Safe Haven: Harry S Truman and the Founding of Israel," historians Allis Radosh

History

and Ronald Radosh survey Truman's efforts to resolve the nettlesome Palestine dilemma that he inherited from Franklin D. Roosevelt. Given Truman's thin and unimpressive record on Jewish affairs, American Jewish leaders had reason for concern about the new president's views. As a U.S. senator, he had delivered one notable speech about the annihilation of European Jewry, at a rally in Chicago in 1943. The Radoshes call it "Truman's greatest expression of sympathy for the plight of Europe's Jews," but it appears to have been his only significant expression of sympathy on the subject. Of greater consequence (although not mentioned in "A Safe Haven") was Truman's cold reply, that same year, to a constituent who urged him to press for the rescue of Jewish refugees: "I do not think it is the business of Senators who are not on the Foreign Relations Committee to dabble in matters which affect our relations with the Allies at this time." There were, of course, various personal factors in Truman's background that may have played a role in shaping his perspective on Jewish matters. The Radoshes, like others who have written on Truman and Israel, point to his childhood love for Bible stories and his friendship and business ventures with Jewish haberdasher Eddie Jacobson. On the other hand, Truman's diaries and private correspondence were littered with arguably anti-Semitic remarks; the Radoshes quote several of these, but do not regard them as having influenced his policies.

As president, Truman's seesawing policies on immigration to Palestine and the creation of a Jewish state left American Jews bewildered. One day, a Truman promise would fill them with hope; the next day, a contradictory remark or hint from the president would leave them reeling with disappointment. American Zionist leaders who met Truman shortly after he became president in 1945 were pleased by his assurance that he was "sympathetic to the Zionist cause." Just a few weeks later, however, Truman sent private letters to Arab leaders reiterating FDR's pledge to take no action on Palestine without first consulting the Arabs. The Radoshes believe he did so under the sway of the strongly pro-Arab State Department, and "without thinking too much about it," although it seems surprising that a president would affix his signature to documents on such a crucial foreign policy question without some discussion or understanding of what he was signing. At a press conference on his way home from the Potsdam conference that summer, Truman said he wanted to "let as many of the Jews into Palestine as is possible." But soon afterward there were press reports that he privately told a congressman that, while he favored Jewish immigration, "he was afraid that Arab opposition would be too great" and therefore he would prefer to focus on "Jewish rights in Europe." Would the real Harry Truman please stand up? Truman endorsed the recommendation by the Harrison Report (1945) and the Anglo-American Committee of Inquiry on Palestine (1946) that 100,000 Holocaust survivors be admitted to Palestine. But he resisted putting serious pressure on the British to allow this recommendation to be fulfilled, and rejected American Zionists' proposal to link Britain's request for a postwar U.S. loan to changes in its immigration policy. In the autumn of 1946, Truman for the first time declared, albeit very tentatively, his support for the creation of a small Jewish state in Palestine. The following year, he endorsed the United Nations plan to partition Palestine into Jewish and Arab states. But the shift of America's position would have been more significant had it been accompanied by practical steps to implement it.

The Radoshes suggest, with justification, that Truman's endorsement of Jewish statehood was to some extent a response to British and Arab intransigence. England's adamant refusal to admit the 100,000 Holocaust survivors to Palestine and the Arab world's unyielding rejection of a Jewish state of any size left him precious little room to maneuver. Had the British or the Arabs been willing to compromise at all, Truman might well have embraced some solution short of statehood. Their inflexibility, combined with tremendous domestic political pressure in support of Zionism, left him with little choice. The significance attributed to that domestic pressure in shaping Truman's policies is one of the key differences between "A Safe Haven" and earlier works on the subject, such as Michael Cohen's 1991 book, "Truman and Israel" (Univ. of California Press). Prof. Cohen provided a small mountain of evidence showing that Truman's major decisions on Palestine policy were profoundly influenced by electoral considerations. The gubernatorial race in New York in 1945, the crucial midterm congressional elections in 1946, and of course Truman's own presidential race in 1948, all loomed large as the president and his advisers weighed possible solutions to the Palestine conflict. The Radoshes acknowledge private statements made by Truman and his aides during 1945-1948 indicating that the potential loss of Jewish votes in New York was a major factor in policymaking on Palestine. At the same time, they also present postwar statements by Truman and several advisers vehemently denying the role of domestic electoral pressure. As evidence that concern about Jewish votes was not a central factor in Truman's Mideast policymaking, the Radoshes offer the interesting example of the president's decision not to grant de jure recognition to Israel in the fall of 1948, even though doing so might have helped him with Jewish voters. (The de facto recognition Truman granted the previous May had been a tentative step acknowledging that Israel controlled certain territory; de jure recognition meant extending full recognition to Israel's existence as a matter of principle.) By the same logic, the Radoshes might have also argued that Truman's refusal to end the U.S. arms embargo in the fall of 1948 demonstrated his lack of concern about the Jewish vote. Yet the Radoshes do not present evidence that, in the autumn of 1948, Truman's advisers urged these pro-Israel steps in order to secure Jewish votes (as they had prior to his recognition of Israel the previous May). They do quote a Democratic gubernatorial candidate in Connecticut warning Truman that he could lose that state if he did not extend de jure recognition - but Connecticut, with just six electoral votes, was not New York, which had 47.

An alternative explanation could be that Truman was unwilling to - as congressman Celler put it - "go the full way" in supporting Israel in the fall of 1948 simply because he did not perceive it as politically necessary. He calculated - correctly - that most Jewish voters would support him out of gratitude for his de facto recognition of Israel and would overlook other issues. Why should he pick a fight with his own State Department, not to mention the Arab world, over such issues if his political advisers were not counseling him that they were necessary for his election? The Radoshes conclude that "If FDR had lived and Truman not been president, there probably would not have been an Israel." This raises an interesting question, but the answer depends on what one sees as the key factors in bringing about Israel's creation. If one accepts the premise that Truman's support for bringing 100,000 Jewish immigrants to Palestine and establishing a small Jewish state there played a significant role in the creation of Israel, and that his recognition of Israel helped it survive the 1948 Arab invasion, then Truman's role looms large indeed. If, however, one believes that 50 years of immigration, swamp-draining and town-building, four years of armed revolt against the British, and a valiant war of self-defense (waged largely with Soviet-bloc weapons) were of greater significance, then Truman's record - whatever his motives - may have received more credit than it deserves.

To the left the grin of a suffering man, Gerald Ford. With his consciously malicious intervention in the Warren Commission report (concerning the exact place where the last bullet hit the president), he lied to deceive.

"I lied for the sake of the American people, not to distort the truth", he later had to confess publicly. Still today it amazes me that Ford managed to force the word "truth" through his rotten throat. The above picture shows Ford's least cynical look I could find on the web. Dear voter, from wherever on the globe you proceed: do not believe a politician for his candid smile, nor for his beautiful tie.

President Bush took his oath of office on the George Washington Bible which belongs to St. Johns Lodge in New York City. Because the Bible belonged to a Masonic Lodge many writers assumed he was a Freemason. Other presidents who took their oath of office with this Bible are Warren G. Harding, Dwight D. Eisenhower and Jimmy Carter.

On pages 44 and 45 of Bill Clinton's best-selling autobiography, "My Life", published by Alfred A. Knopf publishers, New York, in 2004, President Clinton speaks about his involvement with, and attitude towards,

History

Freemasonry and DeMolay, a masonic youth group. As you will see, he is favorable toward both, and makes a specific favorable mention of Prince Hall Masons, too.

In Skull and Bones, Chapter 322, on reads "Behold, the man has become as one of us (us is not the creator of all but the fallen ones) gods—Man has become as one of us to know what is good and what is evil". That leaves little doubt about the illuminati Bush's being freemasons, too. The urban dictionary mentions the following:

> The number 322 that figures on the "Skull and Bones" emblem, stands for Chapter 322 of the "Illuminati Germaniae". At Yale University, the group was founded in 1832 by Phi Beta Kappa pledges William Huntington Russell and Alphonso Taft. 1 The first Skull and Bones class, or "cohort," was the very next year, 1832-33. The society was all male until 1992. The Russell Trust Association is the business name for the New Haven, Connecticut based Skull and Bones society, incorporated in 1856. In 1943, by special act of the Connecticut state legislature, its trustees were granted an exemption from filing corporate reports with the Secretary of State, which is normally a requirement. The business and political network of the Skull and Bones is well detailed

by Hoover Institution scholar Antony Sutton in the expose America's Secret Establishment. Social organizations connected to the Russell Trust covert activities network include Bohemian Grove (a 2700 acre redwood forest, located in Monte Rio, CA) and Deer Island Club (Tavares Fl, 32778), which also operate as corporations. Many influential figures have been in Bones, and influential families have often had multiple members over successive generations. Bonesmen range from U.S. Presidents such as Prescott Bush, George H. W. Bush, and William Howard Taft along with Supreme Court Justices, business leaders and U.S. Both John Kerry and George W. Bush were members of Skull and Bones. They refused to talk about their common membership in Skull and Bones, despite being asked on television about it. Bush: "It's so secret I can't talk about it." Interviewer: "What does that mean for America?" Bush refused to answer that question. In another interview, when Kerry was in turn asked what could he reveal about Skull and Bones, Kerry said: "Well not much, because it's a secret... Sorry, I wish there was something I could manifest".

History

Barack Obama is a manifest freemason, although neither the Grand Lodge of Illinois nor the Prince Hall Grand Lodge of Illinois have any record that Obama was made a freemason. Obama has never said that he was a freemason. There are no photographs of him in Masonic regalia. However, he gave away too many freemasonic clues to make his denial credible.[43]

I have no sufficient information about Donald Trump. As far as I know, Trump never donated to Illuminati organizations, never visited masonic temples nor participated in masonic rites. Moreover, many of his political decisions rather disturb the freemasons.

What I do know, is that all 33rd degree freemasons promote, among others, satanic child abuse and marriage infidelity. They have to pay their ascension to the highest level by offering their own children. Every child (mostly daughters) of such a monster can confirm this.[44] This is the best brainwashing therapy for those children ever following their parents' footsteps, by the way: many 33rd level freemasons were severely abused of in their youth.

---

[43] http://www.blessedquietness.com/journal/housechu/barak_obama_freemason.htm

[44] E.g., Evonne shares her testimony of how, raised by a mother (daughter of the eastern star) and father (33rd degree freemason), she endured satanic ritual abuse: https://ntka.org/cebte/sra-survivor-evonne-dad-was-33rd-degree-freemason_OFQSkfcAYDY.html. Note that all these pages are virus-infected.

CHAPTER 2

Statistics

2.1 Third World Countries

From the site "lovinadoptin" is the following schematic, with statistics from "childhelp":

These shocking numbers proceed from India.

Chapter 2

They differ in those from first world countries in their parental abuse (often due to poverty-caused lack of living space) and their being a "market" of unprotected children.

Statistics

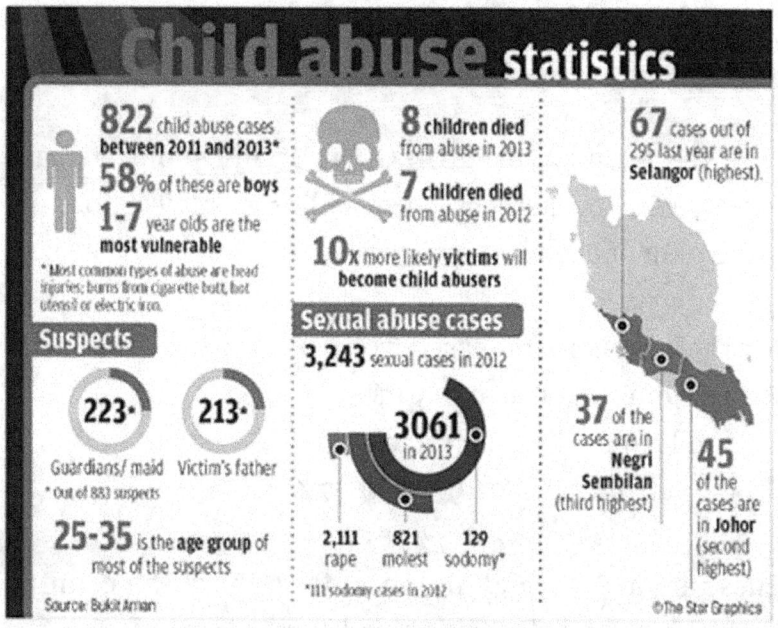

The above data for Malaysia show that, possibly like in India, many abused children have been sodomized. It is horrible, but not surprising, that a sodomized victim is 10 times more prone to being a child abuser than average.

2.2 First World Countries

Over the period 2000-2018 Great Britain shows a steady increase in the percentage of children subject to child protection plans or on registers:

Northern Ireland increased from 0. 35 % to 0.50%
Wales from   0. 29% to 0.50%
England from   0.23% to 0.43%
Scotland from   0.19% to 0.27%

These are awfully high numbers for a European country, though extremely low for a third-world country.

Statistics   47

The poster below warns for taking the 0.5% percentage for granted, due to the many not registered victims of child abuse.

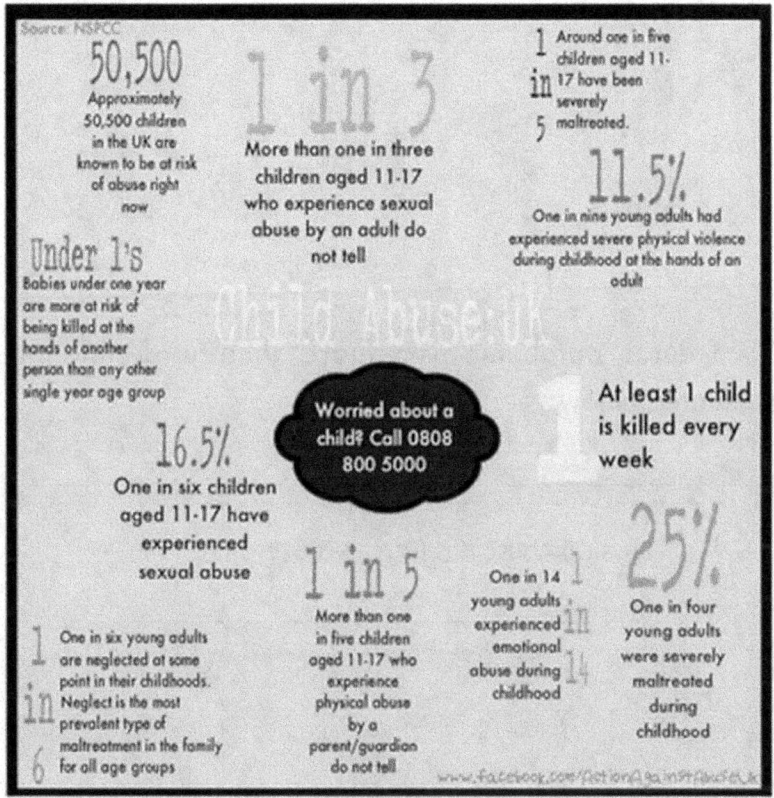

We now turn to the USA. Possibly superfluous to mention: but the baby victims under 1 year rise exponentially.

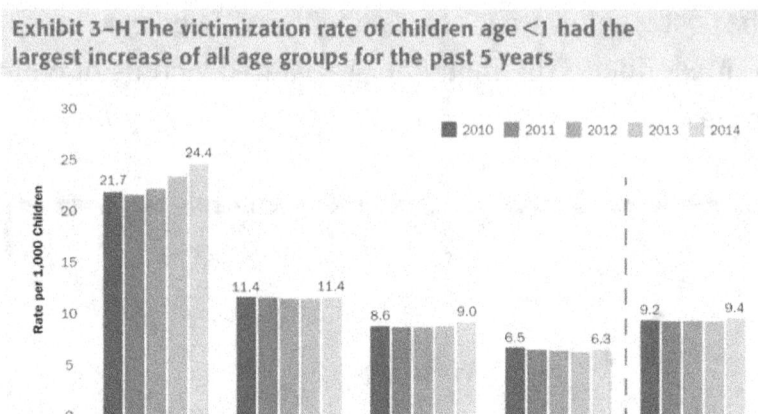

US federal numbers over more than a decade are presented below:

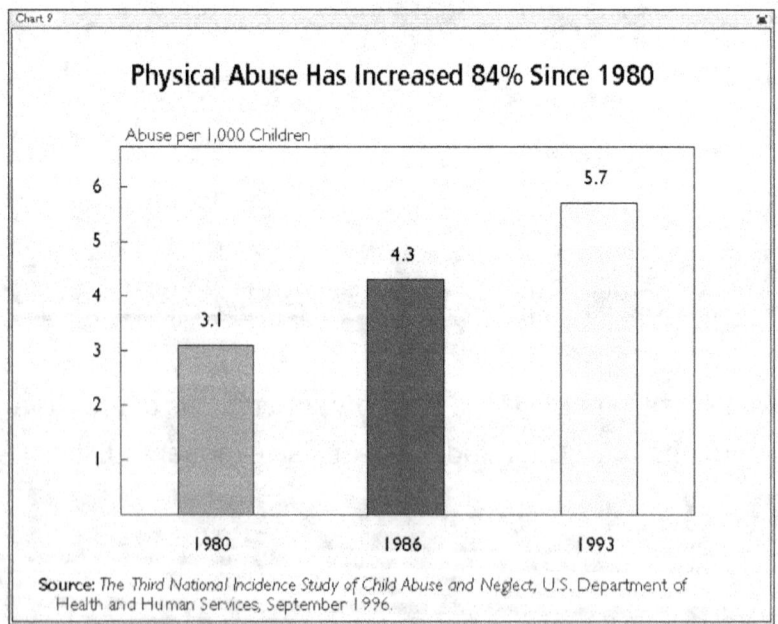

Statistics

These numbers show a nonlinearly increasing trend, which might extrapolate to about 2% in 2019 for physical abuse only! If the extrapolation were somewhere close to truth, for sure the pertinent numbers cannot be published any more. They would cause a nation-wide panic.

According to Rainn only 7% of the abusers are strangers:

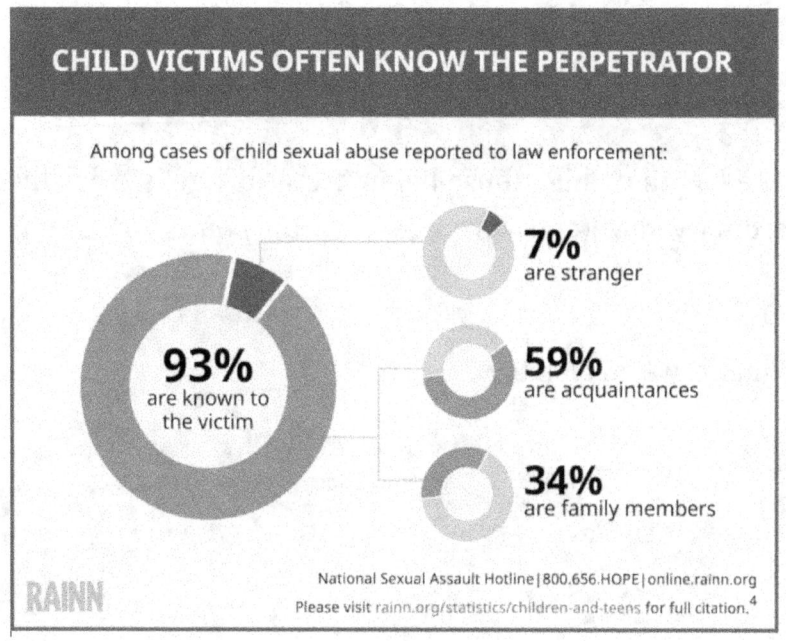

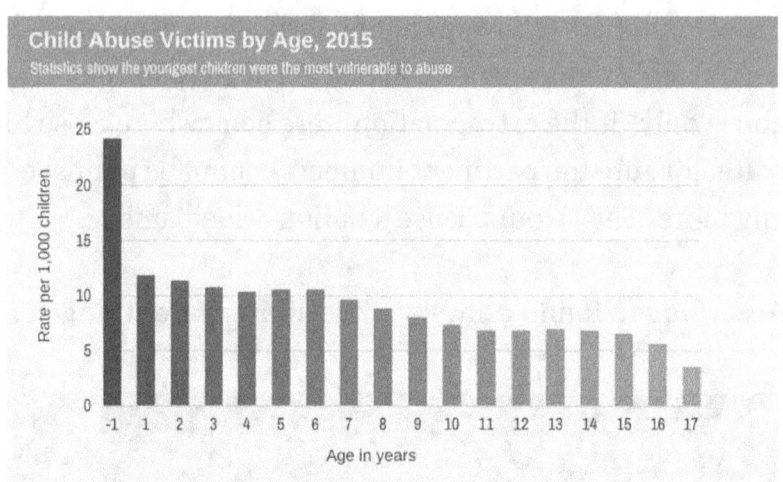

The fact that child abuse below 1 year of age is twice the ordinary rate (above 1 year) *directly points at satanic ritual offerings.*

Finally, we go global.

Statistics

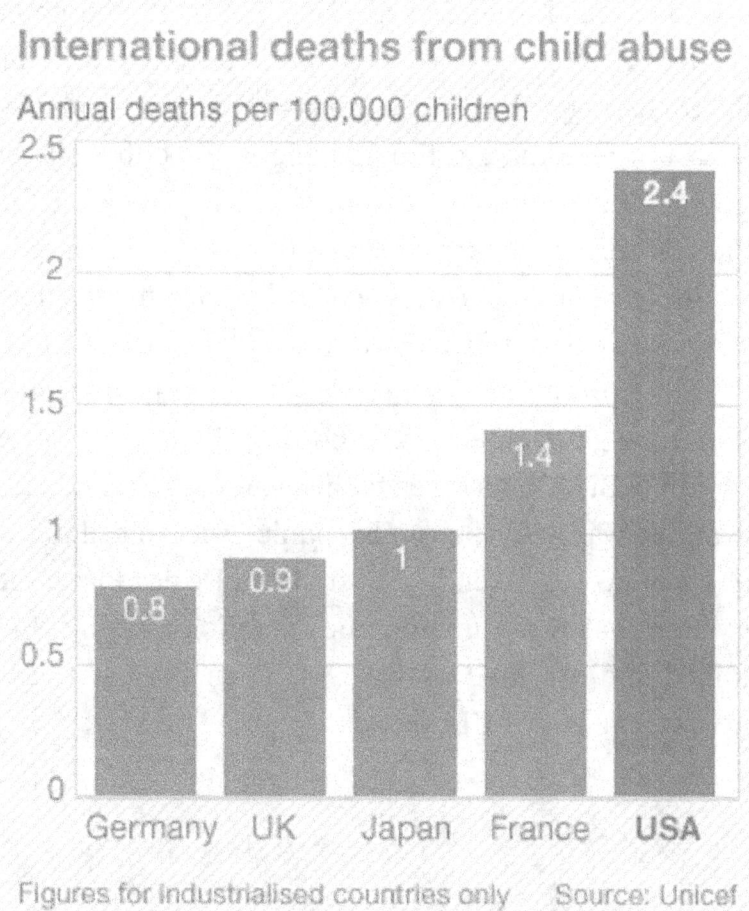

The bar graph above compares four rich countries. Too bad the children's age is not mentioned in this graph, but sure the trade in babies aged under 1, is big business in industrialized countries. The amount of poor immigrants is getting so high that the same rich countries do not need to go in search for those babies abroad anymore.

As I mentioned somewhere else, the right honorable president G.W.H. Bush sr. was specialized in setting up baby trade rings. The connection is simple: if you are CIA, the easiest way tho get things done is to confront your victims with the photo's taken when they were in full action. Moreover, it provides an attractive profit margin, that always comes in handy when the government does not approve of some CIA proposals. Certainy, when added to the drug profits, one may set up any program one likes, without the government ever knowing about it. However honorable Bush's services to his country might be, a coward he was and is, given his panic-stricken call to the CIA when he was taken into custody on Dealey Plaza, the very hour that JFK was shot. The operation was no doubt planned and executed by the CIA. Even the patsy, Lee Harvey Oswald, was CIA.[45]

---

[45] For proof see "Patriotic Ingenuousness" and "The Snake".

2.3 Marriage

Marriage is not a feature that was popular in the Middle Ages. It is the very foundation of society. just have a look at this graph:[46]

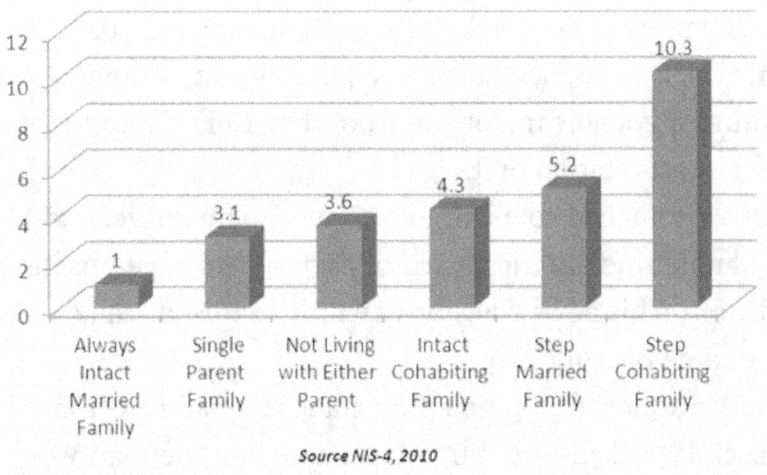

Relative Rates of Physical Abuse by Family Structure

Source NIS-4, 2010

---

[46] As usual, the NIS sillybillies do not know that 'rates' *by definition* refer to temporal derivatives of time-dependent quantities. The present quantities are called, in all scientific disciplines, "population fractions" instead, unless "per year" is *explicitly* mentioned. Now, nobody knows what the NIS numbers exactly refer to.

The bar graph above gives a shocking insight into the causal relation of the parental bonding and child victims. Hence, young mothers, be aware: your newly acquired friend is 10 times more likely to abuse of your daughter than the natural father, whatever his vices might be. If your friend is psychologically normal, he will take advantage of your daughter when she is around 14. If he's not, he will do it when she is under 1.

This graph clearly shows why marriage should be taken more seriously. Not so much the modern concept of it, which is applicable to any possible way humans and animals cohabit under one roof, but Christ's 2000-year old interpretation of it.

He attached so much importance to marriage, that He did not mind another batch of party-goers to get insanely drunk on his new provision of wine (an episode called "the wedding of Cana").

He attached so much importance to marriage, that his disciples asked him: but what mentally sane man would ever marry under your conditions? *Read that, my dear heathen, and never forget why the reason that women are treated less badly in cultures stemming from Christendom than in any other.*

Sure, in our enlighted society women are supposed to be equal sex-chasers as men. A lie as Judas. The reason is mere evolutionary: women pay having sex with pregnancy, giving birth, and having at least 18 hard years of educational efforts that are not even acknowledged by the husband, let alone by society.

Sure again, using our pharmacetic contraception, women can get rid of their conceived baby. Is that not a tremendous advancement? In order to only have their lust granted, women are degraded from property (as they were BC) to mere sexual lust-providing machines. Congratulations, women! Of course, if you really wish so, you can sink even deeper.[47]

2.4 Conspicuously Absent

Although some graphs of section 2.1 point it out clearly, the big danger is not in the big numbers, and certainly not in the high percentage of abused children who already know their abuser (93%). It is obviously excellent to point this out, in order to warn single mothers that her new boyfriend statistically belongs to the highest risk category of child abusers: whatever he says or promises.

But what is the mother's alternative? To stay single and raise her daughter in heaven-claiming poverty? No

---

47 See "Feminine Feminist" for alternative proposals.

accusation from my side, for single mothers who take the risk. So let us concentrate on the smaller numbers.

The smallest number of all numbers, the 7% child abusers that are *unknown to the child*, is the most significant one. Those are the ones this book's investigation is devoted to. *Those are the newborns that are killed in satanic rituals.* However, extremely few studies treat these cases. The reason is simple: the performers of satanic rituals are the most powerful people on earth: the international Sadducee or EZ mafia, and their 33rd degree freemason mercenaries.

Chapter 3

Survivors

3.1 Great Britain

Originally aired in 1989 by Australian 60-minute journalist Ian Leslie: British Theresa is a 15 years old survivor of satanic abuse. She tells Ian that satan was called lucifer. He was to be pleased by killing newborns, 4-year olds, and even adults.[48] She remembered one laughing all the time[49] until they pushed a knife into his body. They slowly killed him, while he was screaming out loud. Teresa was 11 when she conceived her first child. She had about 7 pregnancies. Her babies were aborted by in-house doctors. The fetuses were sometimes killed in front of her, and *Theresa was made to eat her own fetus by pressure of her own grandma.* For not being able to cope with her kids, Theresa's mother had to leave her two kids

---

[48] https://www.youtube.com/watch?v=rvd_MhrWp9g
[49] He was obviously drugged and unaware of his fate

to her father. Theresa comments that during her satanic prison time, some twenty other children were imprisoned with her. The bodies of the dead were burnt until total disappearance.

3.2 Australia

Fiona Barnett is a very trustworthy witness of a VIP satanic ritual in Bathurst, 1985 under the banner of "The Order of the Eagle".[50] VIP's present were, Richie Benaud (BBC, Australian News Personality & His Birthday), Kim Beazley Senior (Politician, Communist Party Member), Bruce Spence (Actor, Communist and Freemason), John Avery (Head of NSW Police at the time), and other notable people. Fiona was brought here by her handler, Dr. Leonas Petrauskas (Russian Theosophist and Rosicrucian). She comments:

> So there was this heavily pregnant woman. They laid here down. Everybody laughing, except me, of course. She was not hypnotized, not drugged, and screaming out loud, with

---

[50] https://www.youtube.com/watch?v=87lRjfLg2Sk

adrenaline bursting down her veins. Then came this priest, with his usual invocation to, you know, baal, lucifer, hail satan, son of the morning. (...)Then he lifts his knife, and cuts her belly open from the diaphragm down to the pelvic bone, and blood just, pisses, everywhere, it's like a waterfall, everywhere, and then, they pulled the baby out, and, there are people assisting, and they've got, a gold platter, and they've got, a, gold chalice, and they collect the blood, of the baby, they drain the baby's blood, in the chalice, and they chop the baby up, and put it on the gold platter, and then they pass it around for "Holy Communion", so it's the black mass, where the Catholic Mass is based on, so nothing Christian about the Catholic Mass.[51] And the next thing I remember is, they lined up, this line of children, who must have been about, they looked about 8, 9, 10 years, that sort of thing, they had them lined up on the stage, and they were hypnotized, and the children did nothing and stared straight ahead, and they were very attractive children [Fiona

---

51 I beg to differ

starts weeping, but controls herself] and they had a samurai sword, it was incredibly sharp, and he ritually slices off the head of each child.

3.3 United States of America

As a little girl, Nancy Dunn was used to "breed" babies for her father to sacrifice in his rituals as a satanist high priest.[52] At very young age, she was sexually abused by her father, and forced to witness satanic rites. After her eleventh, her babies were used for her father's satanic rituals. Once adult, her parents let her loose. She started a disbanded life, and chose for a clinical abortion. She was diagnosed Dissociative Identity Disorder (DID): she had flashbacks so severe that she had split into several personalities in order to cope with the trauma. She finally found rest in Born-Again Christianity. There, it took her 18 months to bring together her compartmentalized memories into a single person's memories. Still she was not healed. That happened instantaneously, when she drank Jesus' Eucharistic Blood: something very hard for

---

52 https://www.youtube.com/watch?v=ZOj76xrG62k

her, as she was used to drinking natural, human blood. When speaking to God about her troubles with drinking Jesus' Eucharistic Blood, He told her His Blood would *instantly* heal her from all her trauma's. And so it happened. Shortly before her father died, she forgave him everything. Whereupon her father said: Nancy, I found God, too. Nancy was not satisfied: she asked him to say Jesus' prayer out loud with her, and he did so. A few minutes later, he died. Nancy comments: and now he is in Heaven.

    I was surprised to see Nancy speaking out her first sentences in the interview. She looks like a perfectly normal woman, attractive, and pain-free. However, later in the interview, her face sometimes betrays the extreme torture she endured in her childhood. I guess this is nothing short of a miracle.

Dellena, from California, suffered penetration by a dog.[53]

Jay Parker's parents were member of a three centuries old illuminati family.[54] He does not speak much about his child SRA (satanic ritual abuse) experiences, apart from saying that he once was buried alive. He also limits himself to speaking of sodomizing little children, not of

---

53 https://www.youtube.com/watch?v=OntjTAsfhpo
54 https://youtu.be/chyEyMs1_d8

ritually sacrificing them. *Yet he is the only survivor I know of that links SRA to global wars, to Christian stupidity, and to JFK's assassination.*

As you might know from other books in my decalogue, wars are necessary, not only to fill the Sadducees' pockets (who lend huge amounts of money to both contestants), but also to provide cults with large reservoirs of people suffering post-traumatic stress disorder (PTSD) and DID. Jay Parker applies this directly to World War I and II. Moreover, according to Jay Parker, in the US, PTSD occurs on large scale with in vitro babies, due to the use of periodic shock therapy. Luckily for him, Jay Parker firmly believes in the thorough goodness of this world, as being a creation of God the Father, and us being liberated by the Holy Ghost.

> JP: Who went to jail for lying to us and getting us into the war in Iraq?
>
> Interviewer: nobody.
>
> JP: Did anybody even get called out on it? Did they have congressional hearings on it? (…) The majority of people on earth are good! (…) My mother said the cultists [followers of the "old

Survivors 63

religion"][^55] were 12% in 1963. I don't know if the cult's gotten bigger. It certainly looks that way by looking at society. When you look at Madonna, Lady Gaga, Spirit Cooking,[^56] Hollywood, eating cakes that look like bodies... That's just job of Dustin [Pedroia] and the pedophile art of him and his brother [Brett]. I'm tired of these people.

Interviewer: Do you think some of those people connected with James Alifantism, may have been illuminati?

JP: Are you kidding? absolutely! Pedophilia is a *sacrament* in the old religion. Once you have a [sic] entity[^57] attack you when you decide to go cult, the entity has to, feed, on the life worth, of the child, through you raping it. That's how the entity lives, in this space. So you're part of the demons for the rest of your life when you go cult. (...) [The illuminati] control everything

---

[^55]: Ancient Phoenicia, Ancient Canaan, Ancient Babylon some 4000 years ago
[^56]: Look up Serbian performance artist Marina Abramović on the web, and the accusation for using it at the address of Hillary Clinton and John Podesta.
[^57]: As I understand JP, "the entity" stands for the satan

in our lives through the main stream media. Television pours out subliminal messages continuously. Internet is going to save the world. That provides an alternative source of communication that the illuminati still do not control. See us here, for example, talking.

Interviewer: Isn't it important for people to know about these cults?

JP: Well, sure, I tell them what I know about them. But I care much more about how to turn this ship around, rather than peeling off the onion. There's so many layers to it. Like with JFK: was the mob involved? Then the CIA? Then the government? (...) Don't you see that America has had only ten years of peace since its foundation? Well, in the beginning, this was tolerated, as crime was directed against American natives. *Our nation is built on blood.* (...) Trump cut tens of thousands of regulations! Why? To get rid of the bureaucracy, of the totalitarian control! He got rid of TPP, I mean, he's really trying to get back American sovereignty, and American rule of law. Since he got office, some 8400 pedophiles have been arrested![58] (...) You know, an entire generation is being lobotomized. Do you really need 80 vaccinations to survive? 80? (...) Harry Weinstein and Congress perverts: do you know how many CEO's have retired since Trump took office? Some 50 major CEO's. (...) Since the 1978 banking act the US became a corporation. *America is under the rule of pedophiles.* The police (they were actually crying) looking at Weiner's tapes, showing Abe and Hillary raping babies, certainly copied them. Then they sent it to the FBI, saying, if you don't do anything against this, we'll release the files.

---

58 Jay Parker said this November 22nd, 2018

3.4 The Vatican

Most people do not believe in the existence of satanic rituals: atheists, agnostics, theosophists, and so forth. Strangely, this also holds for Christians. They do not have any consistency problems with its existence, but when challenged to talk about it, they refuse, as if the mere possibility makes them sick. Congratulations, I would say, be as sick as you want, add that to your belief in the existence of satan and his cozy hell, and it won't do any harm to your living your Christian virtues. Quite the contrary: all those little offers you don't manage to bring to your God, offers of a broken, penitent heart, they will come much easier. Your faith, your holy wish for reaching sanctity, and your love of God will jump to ever higher levels. If abused people, like Nancy Dunn and Jay Parker, speak out so clearly, what possible doubt can there remain for convinced Christians? Does the Catechism of the Catholic Church not speak as clearly about the existence and permanent actuation of the devil in all people? It seems like Christianity has fallen asleep, Catholicism included. We now have a semi-heretic homosex-indulging Pope sitting on Peter's throne, and no one speaks out but four cardinals. This seems to be a real big issue for many Catholics. I think I understand why: Catholics have never applied Christ's distinction between what Pharisees *teach* and what they *do*, to the very Pope. As far as the Pharisees are concerned, Jesus told his followers to *try to do what they teach, though never to follow what they do*. Indeed, he called them hypocrites and graves (Luke 11:44). Now, dear Catholic, please tell me what the probem is with a not particularly exemplary Pope? Let me offer you a little help. Think of Peter himself: "And the second time the cock crowed. And Peter called to mind the words that Jesus had said unto him (Mark 14:30): "Before the cock crows twice, thou shalt deny Me thrice." And when he thought thereon, he wept (Mark 14:72)". Before that betrayal, the Lord even called him a Satan: "Get thee behind Me, Satan! Thou art an offense unto Me; for thou savorest not the things that be of God, but those that be of men" (Matthew 16:23 and a parrallel in Mark 8:33). Every Pope is, like every other man, a sinner. if he lives a holy life, like e.g. Pope John Paul the Great ("santo subito!"), he only falls 7 times a day, in terms of daily sins. Now how many times would Bergoglio fall a day, in terms of mortal sins? Let us leave it as a merely rhetorical question.

So how does a Catholic need to act in the face of a weak or posessed Pope like Bergoglio? That is quite simple. In order of importance: first, stick to the Pope as the only Divinely appointed follower of St. Peter, pray for him all you can, and do everything he preaches (as long as it is in conformity with the orthodox teachings of the Church), *though never act as he does.*[59] Such a semi-schizophrenic posture towards a single human person is not a simple thing to handle, but it is not impossible, as I prove to you in this very book. If one thinks about it a little more, it is the same "semi-schizophrenia" of empathic mothers who love their children, even when they disobeyed their parents and comitted heavy crimes. I can ony urge male Catholics to concentrate their brains on empathy for a while, rather than on blunt systemizing.

All this being said, it is of prime importance to criticize the Pope whenever he goeas astray in mortal sin. Paul was not even a priest, when he rebuked Peter's hypocrisy in public. Most importantly, those criticisms should always end with a confession of one's submission to the Head of the Church. Indeed, all Popes blundered from their first day until the present, as all are human, and subjet to human weakness. Why do you think Luther had such an impact with his protest against the Roman Church? Certainly not because of his high standard of virtue, nor his large curriculum spent for helping out the needy, nor for anything that really matters. It was not his action that had any influence, but the failure to act of the flock. Who would have taken notice of Luther if he was the thousandth in the line of Catholic protests against the

---

[59] Pope Benedict XVI does not cease to call for the unity of all Catholics under Pope Francis

failing leadership in Rome? Hence, in my view, not to overtly accuse the Pope for failing leadership in special circumstances, can be a mortal sin. And I, for one, am not going to get Bergoglio away with his failures of leadership.

After Bergoglio's election, he immediately cancelled all initiatives started by Pope Benedict XVI:

- preaching Catholic morality
- cleansing the IOR (the Vatican Bank)[60]
- persecuting child abusers within the Catholic clergy
- and installing a Bishops' tribunal for child abuse.

After taking office, Bergoglio's immediate agenda consisted in undoing all five of his predecessor's endeavors.[61]

---

60 See appendix A2
61 Prior to 2001, the primary responsibility for investigating allegations of sexual abuse and disciplining perpetrators rested with the individual dioceses. In 2001, Ratzinger convinced John Paul II to put the Congregation for the Doctrine of the Faith in charge of all investigations and policies surrounding sexual abuse in order to combat such abuse more efficiently. According to John L. Allen, Jr., Ratzinger in the following years "acquired a familiarity with the contours of the problem that virtually no other figure in the Catholic Church can claim" and "driven by that encounter with what he would later refer to as 'filth' in the

Anything but strange, given the typically freemasonic manipulation exerted at his election.[62]

In my personal view, Bergoglio's early claim that he "would enter history as the Pope who split the Church" was a clear sign of his being an EZ marionet.[63] This impression was further confirmed by (i) *the fact that the SWIFT blackmail on Pope Benedict XVI was lifted at the very moment the latter publicly declared to step back*, and (ii) *the fact that Bergoglio used his time, preceding Trump's first election to Presidency, to repeatedly attack Trump's wall initiative*,[64] while never uttering a word of criticism on nazi Hillary, her death squads in Libya, her

---

Church, Ratzinger seems to have undergone something of a 'conversion experience' throughout 2003–04. From that point forward, he and his staff seemed driven by a convert's zeal to clean up the mess". In his role as Head of the CDF, he "led important changes made in Church law: the inclusion in canon law of internet offences against children, the extension of child abuse to include the sexual abuse of all under 18, the case by case waiving of the statute of limitation and the establishment of a fast-track dismissal from the clerical state for offenders." As the Head of the CDF, Ratzinger developed a reputation for handling these cases. According to Charles J. Scicluna, a former prosecutor handling sexual abuse cases, "Cardinal Ratzinger displayed great wisdom and firmness in handling those cases, also demonstrating great courage in facing some of the most difficult and thorny cases, sine acceptione personarum (without exceptions)".

62 That election remains valid, even though one had God's gift of seeing all the cause-effect chain in his election procedure.

63 See "The Snake" by Yitzhak Rosenthal (2019): EZ is the historically continuous follow-up of the Sadducee mafia.

64 nothing different from Obama's

erection of Al-Qaeda, and their multiple terror attacks on European targets. What better marionet could EZ wish?

Afterwards, Bergoglio gets rid of four Dubia authors in an utterly shameful way. He reinstates renowned pedophiles like McCarmick, the late Cardinal Danneels' uncle, Bishop Roger Vangheluwe, and appoints self-declared pedophile Bishop Paglia as his right hand. Paglia's function is apparently to publicly promote homosexuality at the Holy See as a usual subject of jokes. Paglia's jokes are highly appreciated by Italian anti-Catholic VIPs, like the already discussed Benigni.

What a huge difference with Bergoglio's Saintly predecessor! One of the cases Ratzinger pursued, involved Father Marcial Maciel Degollado, a Mexican priest and founder of the "Legion of Christ", accused of multiple sexual abuse. Biographer Andrea Tornielli suggested that Cardinal Ratzinger had wanted to take action against Marcial Maciel Degollado, but that John Paul the Great and high-ranking officials, including several cardinals and notably the Pope's influential secretary Stanisław Dziwisz, prevented him from doing so. According to Jason Berry, Angelo Sodano "pressured" Cardinal Ratzinger, who was "operating on the assumption that the charges were not justified", to halt the proceedings against Maciel in 1999. When Maciel was honored by the John Paul the Great in 2004, new accusers came forward and Cardinal Ratzinger "took it on himself to authorize an investigation of Maciel".

After Ratzinger became pope he began proceedings against Maciel and his "Legion of Christ" that forced Maciel out of active service in the Church. On 1 May 2010 the Vatican issued a statement denouncing Maciel's "very serious and objectively immoral acts", which were "confirmed by incontrovertible testimonies" and represent "true crimes and manifest a life without scruples or authentic religious sentiment." Pope Benedict also said he would appoint a special commission to examine the Legionaries' constitution and open an investigation into its lay affiliate "Regnum Christi". Cardinal Christoph Schönborn explained that Ratzinger "made entirely clear efforts not to cover things up but to tackle and investigate them. This was not always met with approval in the Vatican". According to Cardinal Schönborn, Cardinal Ratzinger had pressed John Paul the Great to investigate Hans Hermann Groër, an Austrian cardinal and friend of John Paul accused of sexual abuse, resulting in Groër's resignation. In March 2010, the Pope sent a Pastoral Letter to the Catholic Church in Ireland addressing cases of sexual abuse by Catholic priests to minors, expressing sorrow, and promising changes in the way accusations of abuse are dealt with. Victim groups claim the Pastoral Letter failed to clarify if secular law enforcement has priority over canon law confidentiality pertaining to internal investigation of abuse allegations. The Pope then promised to introduce measures that would 'safeguard young people in the future' and 'bring to justice' priests who were responsible for abuse. In April, the Vatican issued guidelines on how existing Church law should be implemented. The guideline dictates that "Civil law concerning reporting of crimes... should always be followed." The guideline was intended to follow the norms established by U.S. bishops, but it does not require the reporting of "allegations" or crimes where reporting is not required by law.

Appendices

The appendices to this book are posted on the site

https://matchliterary.com/manichaeism-and-satanic-child-abuse

Its contents are:

Appendix 1   Sexual Abuse in the Catholic Church
Appendix 2   Benedict XVI's sudden resignation

Appendices

Epilogue

Original Sin

E.1 Demonic Cult Offers

Why would demonic cult offers suddenly explode, just now, at the start of the third millennium of Christianity?

First of all, it has been increasing exponentially since the sexual "liberation" of 1968, which may not have been a totally spontaneous popular movement, but altogether was happily rececived by many youngsters. The reason that such a tendency is much more dangerous in modern times than in ancient ones,[65] is that today mafias work as globally as the largest global companies. Mafias actually *are* global companies. The only difference between them and their legal counterparts is that the larger part of the ignorant, mostly morally libertine public, only criticizes the legal firms, as they are clearly recognizable, pay taxes, place ads, and can succesfully be sued in class actions.

---

[65] What united them all was exactly that, the demonic child offers

This enormous reservoir of morally libertine ignorants is the key weakness of a society fighting against abuse, of whatever kind. These ignorant people are no doubt of good will. However, they simply are essentially unable to grasp the idea that evil does not manifest itself as clearly as good does. They reason as follows: I see no sources of evil, so all evil in the world *necessarily has to be attributed to impenetrable institutions like the Catholic Church, oil companies, or those ridiculously small local mafias* that Hollywood uses to poke fun at.[66]

One would think, these libertines are dumb. I do not think they are. I think they were never encouraged to think by themselves. There can be many smart libertines around, but no matter how smart they are, they sucked it from their mothers' breasts to take the media for granted.

An illiterate moral conservative would not do that, because, even though the person in question were illiterate, she would *have learnt since her tenderest youth to doubt* everything the main stream media say or write.

The situation is serious indeed, to date. That is simply because a single mafia (EZ) of ten times the size of the US (in GDP) owns all the mainstream media, and determines how the "commoners" have to think. How easy it is, for whom has no conscience, to place bombs at either side of

---

[66] Think of the many thriller-comedies about Italian mafias, like "The Godfather"

two peacefully coexisting religions, and therewith start a "religious war".

In the thus created confusion, evil can operate quite overtly because everyone is busy waging war on everyone else. The overt truth as that both sides at war are too stupid to conceive that they are being manipulated. Not very surprisingly, EZ has a solid pact with the devil. The latter happens to demand human sacrifices, as he always did, and always shall do.

E.2 The Problem of Theology

All of the above, and human sins in general, are connected to the phenomenon of "Original Sin": Everybody knows from own experiencec, that one often wishes to do good, but fails to do so. The Catholic Church has tried for two millennia to formalize her teaching about it.

As a scientist, I deplore that the large majority of Catholic Theologians, including the recent Holy Popes, are disqualifying themselves as scientists at a rapid pace. From an historical point of view, I admit that theologians started a scientific discipline one full millennium before natural sciences did. So I feel all sympathy for theologians when a scientist, in their eyes but a baby parvenu, intends to educate them concerning the essence of science. My message is: please hear me out before you tear your garments: I believe that theology is a much more difficult discipline than any natural scientific one.

In the 16th and 17th centuries the natural scientific endeavor led to metaphysical insights on the essence of science that theology never had the occasion to discover.[67] Theologians and natural scientists both believe that the ojective of science is the truth. According to natural scientists, the *scientific procedure* consists in

1. trying to obtain the largest and most trustworthy set of measurements, and
2. trying to find the simplest and smallest set of axioms, which explains all the measured data by means of a logic deduction from first principles (axioms).

Natural sciences were able to metaphysically deduce this procedure from their way of working, thanks to the many observational and model-building mistakes. Natural sciences have this advantage over theology, that repeating experiments is always possible.

---

[67] The reader knows that Isaac Newton spent half his time on a recipee for turning ordinary matter into gold. Today, this endeavor is considered as alchemy, as barren of science as reading one's future off one's hand palms.

For the majority of theologians, dogmatic theology has two major procedural stages.

1. In the first stage, the history of a dogmatic topic is studied historically. In the specific case of original sin, this would be the writings of Pelagius and Celestius, Augustine, Thomas Aquinas, Luther, Calvin, and those of the Counterreformation until to date.
2. In a second stage the theologian tries to build a theory based on the Catholic dogmas, the Catholic Church Fathers, and all later Orthodox Catholic theologians, with the explicit endeavor to reach a theological synthesis of the kind of Thomas Aquinas.

The first and most important aspect of these two procedures, is that they have nothing in common: it looks like natural scientists and theologians live on different planets.

Second, contemporary Catholic dogmatic theologians always get caught up in a net of inconsistencies, no matter what topic they discuss. In the context of original sin, on one hand they like the idea of a "limbo", as a "happy place in hell" holding Augustine's aborted children, and on the other, they preach the baptism of desire. Their final conclusion is as pious as it is nonsensical: The Holy Church can only hope and pray for God's Mercy.

Why is this a stupid conclusion? Well, because God's infinite Mercy and Justice are already dogmatically defined. Hence, there is no need of either hope or prayer,[68] for aborted children to go to heaven. It is a neccesity that follows immediately from the way the Holy Church perceives God's infinite Mercy and infinite Justice. So one can ask: how can theologians fall so low? The obvious answer is that they have no idea of a scientific procedure. Since I wrote it down already, I can do no better than rewrite it for the specific scientific discipline of dogmatic theology.

---

[68] It is quite revevaling that the Cathechism of the Catholic Church mentions, totally impertinently, in point **1261**:
As regards children who have died without Baptism, the Church can only entrust them to the mercy of God, as she does in her funeral rites for them. Indeed, the great mercy of God who desires that all men should be saved, and Jesus' tenderness toward children which caused him to say: "Let the children come to me, do not hinder them," allow us to hope that there is a way of salvation for children who have died without Baptism. All the more urgent is the Church's call not to prevent little children coming to Christ through the gift of holy Baptism.
Why is this impertinent? Because the pertinent quote would obviously not be Jesus' tenderness, which is of little dogmatic consequence, but the quote of the children slaughtered by Herod, which are all declared Martyrs by the Liturgy of the Holy Church. This would be Matthew 2:18:
"A voice was heard in Ramah: Lamentation, weeping, and great mourning, Rachel weeping for her children, refusing to be comforted, because they are no more."
I would love to hear a theologian comment sensefully on what seems to me a pile of contradictions.

Original Sin

There we go:

1. try to obtain the largest and most trustworthy set of dogma's, and
2. try to find the simplest and smallest set of axioms, which explains all these dogmas *by means of a logic deduction from first principles (axioms)*.

That is to say (however strange this may sound), in dogmatic theology, dogmas play the role of measurements in natural sciences. In other words, dogmas are not the first principles or axioms of a theory, but they are the final conclusions of a scientific model.

Where *theologians try to build upon dogmas*, and try to unify all kinds of inherently contradictory opinions, *scientists build below dogmas*, and try to find the simplest set of axioms that explain the dogmas. Again in other words, theologians do exactly the opposite thing they actually should be doing.

E.3 Scientific Dogmatic Theology of Original Sin

One might ask how the writer proposes to handle original sin according to the above "natural scientific procedure". With all dogmas at hand, and all possible options expressed in the history of catholic teachers about original sin, this is not an exercise requiring any genius at all. One just has to pick out all their ideas, which are consistent with the dogmas, and try to formulate the tiniest set of first principles (or axioms) from which all dogmas follow by logical deduction. In the following set of axioms, I assume *monogenism, although not of the endogamous (inbreeding) kind.* Some words and a figure might help understanding these concepts.

There always existed a big fuss about polygenism, since the moment biologists found out that the genetic diversity of a strict endogamous descendence of two individuals, some hundreds of thousands of years ago, could not explain the genetic diversity of makind to date (about 10.000 people). I have nothing against polygenism, but a non-endogamous monogenetic solution is so straightforward that it surprises me one never hears about it.

In my view, it is perfectly compatible with the Catholic faith, that we all descend from two original parents, called Adam and Eve in the Old Testament: However, not in an inbred sense. *The non-inbred sense implies God having endowed every child of a human being with a soul, while the inbred sense implies God having endowed every child of two human parents with a soul.* Given that God was able to endow two chimpanzees with a soul, there exists no single theological argument for denying God's ability to endow as many chimpanzees with souls as He likes. An

Original Sin

interspecies progeny may effectively proceed as long as the human species was interbreedable with genetically close chimpanzee species. This mechanism explains the presence of Neanderthal genes in humanity, without there ever having existed a human soul in a Neanderthal with two Neanderthal parents. The below picture shows the latest 600 thousand years of humanoids.[69]

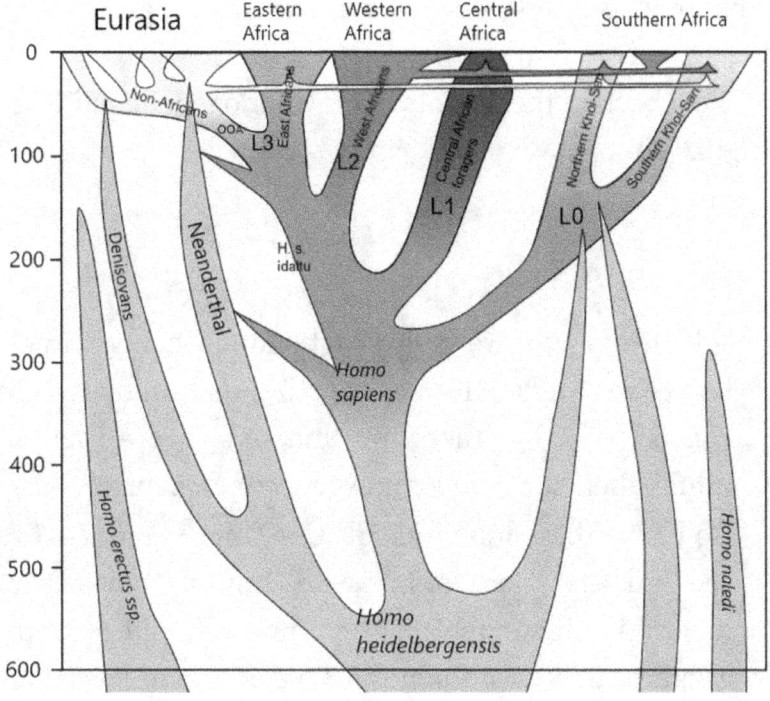

---

[69] https://en.wikipedia.org/wiki/Interbreeding_between_archaic_and_modern_humans

The Church does not know now, nor will ever know as it is on pilgrimige to heaven, when exactly Adam and Eve were converted from chimps into human beings.[70] From a natural scientific point of view, the creation of the first humans must have occurred at least 300 thousand years ago. From then on, there only existed two kinds of humans: those born from inbreed (i.e., from two human parents) and those born from a single human parent and a chimpanzee. This is in full agreement with all Catholic dogmas on original sin.

Now back to the axioms of our monogenetic model of original sin:

- Adam and Eve were the first human beings. Their bodies were taken from chimpanzee-like animals. God converted two of them into humans by creating, ab nihilo, their souls, one for every human being.
- God gave these human souls the "amazing graces" to see God face to face, to talk with Him, to enjoy eternal life, to dominate one's bodily impulses, and so forth. Thereto, God gave them the Tree of Life to feed their

---

[70] Poor fools who take offence at this. The Christ Himself said God had the power to make God's children out of stones. Remember?

Original Sin

bodies, and the Tree of Morality to feed their souls. The latter spiritual anti-food consisted in *not eating from that tree, as a sign of perpetual submission to God.*

- Adam and Eve did however eat from the fruit of the Tree of Knowledge of Good and Bad, hence sinning gravely against the Lord. This sin is called the original sin, and it is a sin of nobody but Adam and Eve.
- As a punishment for their sins, God took away a number of "amazing graces". These graces were not personal graces, bestowed as they were onto both Adam and Eve; but they were graces bestowed onto the nature of mankind. As the humanity had been lowered in grace, it would have become nearly impossible for the children of Adam and Eve to get into Heaven. This is strictly incompatible with God's Mercy. *However, instead of leaving human nature on a comparable level as that of Adam and Eve before their personal sin, God decided to lift the bruised human nature far beyond the original human nature!*[71] The special gift was the Incarnation of the Second Person of the Divine Trinity. As the bruise corresponded to human nature, and not to individuals, likewise the Incarnation corresponded

---

[71] This makes Catholic Liturgy sing "O felix culpa" ("Oh happy guilt") at Easter, the very climax of Christ's death on the cross.

not to individuals, but to all members of the human species.

To these four axioms, one has to add the metaphysical axioms of human freedom as described in "Deism versus Theism". These do not represent the Metaphysics of orthodox Catholic philosophers, as they have no idea about sciencec, either. The resulting system of axioms explains all dogmas by mere logical deduction, except the biblical account of Eve having been formed from Adam's rib.

By way of conclusion, whatever orthodox Catholic theologians try to sell you, do not believe a single word of it. Most of it is self-contradictory and makes no sense at all. And as long as there is no community-broad agreement on original sin, one should desist from studying far more difficult details like that of the difference between man and woman.[72] Very likely, all of it is junk, because man and woman share human nature in exactly the same way. *This means that by mere logic, the*

---

[72] For sure, Paul's texts on the analogy between a Matrimony and the love that Christ has for his Church, form an excellent "scientific measurement", as does Christ's first miracle, on a decisive and unchallengeable request of Our Lady, on the occasion of a wedding turning dry.

roles of man and woman in society have nothing to do with original sin. I do not doubt that their bodily differences reflect societal differences, but as long as theologians do not get their scientific method right, there is little wisdom to be expected from that side of the ballpark. Then, the most "trustworthy measurements" would be the words of Saints, but of course, even Saints might be wrong.

A good example of such a Saint is Augustine from Hippo. Of everything he wrote about original sin, not much more than half of it is true. This is perfectly compatible with the fact that he was God's elected instrument to counter Pelagianism, by introducing the new concept of "grace conferred to human nature". One simply may not expect a genius to invent a completely unknown concept ("grace conferred to human nature", as opposed to "grace conferred to an individual", as occurs in Sacraments), and rightaway start teaching about it in a perfectly consistent way.

I would like to conclude this booklet with a tentative remark on Adam, Eve, and Our Lady. Theology normally assumes Our Lady and her Son to be the antitypes of Adam and Eve, and rightly so.[73] But there is also a big

---

[73] Romans 5,15: "But the free gift is not like the offense. For if by the one man's offense many died, much more the grace of God and the gift by the grace of the one Man, Jesus Christ, abounded to many"

similarity: They were all four created without original sin. While Adam and Eve messed it all up, the Immaculate Virgin, who was as free to sin as were Adam and Eve before their fall, *did not sin even once in her life*, thereby making Incarnation possible.

www.ingramcontent.com/pod-product-compliance
Lightning Source LLC
Chambersburg PA
CBHW052102070526
44584CB00017B/2304